I HAVE A HORSE...
NOW WHAT?

How Grooming, Training, Riding,
and Equine Competitive Activities
Can Build a Lifelong Bond

MEREDITH HILL

© 2022 I Have a Horse... Now What: How Grooming, Training, Riding, and Equine Competitive Activities Can Build a Lifelong Bond

All rights reserved. No part of the book may be reproduced in any shape or form without permission from the publisher.

This guide is written from a combination of experience and high-level research. Even though we have done our best to ensure this book is accurate and up to date, there are no guarantees to the accuracy or completeness of the contents herein.

ISBN: 978-1-953714-52-7

DOWNLOAD YOUR FREE CHECKLIST NOW!

Horse owners are often accused of having too much stuff, and yet we always find ourselves without that One Thing that we really, really need. This list is intended to keep the new horse owner organized so you have a head start on your own collection of "stuff."

Scan this code to download it for free

ALSO BY MEREDITH HILL

Before Your Horse Comes Home   Finding Your First Horse

CONTENTS

Reviews	3
INTRODUCTION	7
PART 1: GETTING TO KNOW YOUR HORSE	13
Section 1: Salutations and Greetings	17
Chapter 1 : An Introduction to Introductions	18
Chapter 2 : Reach out and Touch Your Horse	21
Chapter 3 : Building Friendship through Groundwork	24
Chapter 4 : What If My Horse Doesn't Like Me?	29
Author's Anecdote- Thawing the Ice Princess	34
Section 2 : Deciding What to Do with Your Horse	39
Chapter 1 : What Do You Want to Do?	40
Chapter 2 : What Does Your Horse Want to Do?	44
Chapter 3 : What Is Realistic for Both of You?	47
Author's Anecdote- Red's Very Specific List of Demands	51
PART 2 : AN INTRODUCTION TO EQUINE SPORTS AND ACTIVITIES	55
Section 1 : The English Disciplines	57
Chapter 1 : Riding on the Flat	59
Chapter 2 : Dressage	61
Chapter 3 : Jumping	66
Hunter Jumpers	67
Show Jumping	69
Cross Country / Three Day Eventing	71
Field Hunting	75
Section 2 : The Western Disciplines	79
Chapter 1 : Pleasure and Patterns	81
Western Pleasure	81
Horsemanship	83
Trail	85
Ranch Work	87
Western Dressage	88
Chapter 2 : High Performance Western Sports	90
Reining	91
Speed Events	92
With Bovine Assistance	95
Section 3 : Fun for Everyone	99
Saddleseat and Gaited Horses	100
Going the Distance	102
A Different View Between the Horse's Ears	105
You Don't Have to Ride	106
CONCLUSION	109

RESOURCES	113
Bonding and Communication Work	114
English Riding	114
Riding on the Flat	115
Show Jumping	115
Cross Country / Three Day Eventing	116
Field Hunting	116
Western Riding	117
Overview	117
Pleasure	117
Horsemanship	117
Trail	118
Ranch Riding	118
Western Dressage	118
Reining	119
Speed Events	119
Cowboy Mounted Shooting	120
Cattle Events	120
Other Sports and Activities	120
Saddle Seat	120
Endurance	121
Trail Riding and Competitive Trail Riding	121
Driving	122
Halter and In-Hand	122
Breed Organizations	123

INTRODUCTION

I have had sole responsibility over many horses in my life. If you read the first book in this series, *Before Your Horse Comes Home: Introductory Horse Care for Beginners,* you've already been introduced to my first horse and our bittersweet short story together. But there have been other horses since then. Dolly went on to be a field hunter for a young girl. Maxwell, the ancient Appaloosa, became a family pet after the youngest son fell in love with him. There was Jacob, the naughty eventer who had plenty of brains but very few good ideas. Then, there was the accidental thoroughbred I bought from an internet ad while I was out of town. Today, I enjoy the company of Red, a rescued racehorse I bought for $10 and a hug, and Belle, a registered Quarter Horse who would like everyone to appreciate that she is a princess.

One of the top questions I'm asked about horses is, "What do you do with them all?" My answer surprises people: I enjoy them. People then respond with the following questions, "Do you take them to competitions? Do you have a lot of ribbons?" I have taken them to competitions, yes. I have a fair amount of ribbons. But in my case, it's not about competition; instead, it's about having fun.

I was raised in a very "non-horsey" home. That is to say, my parents weren't exactly keen about my enthusiasm for large, stinky beasts who could potentially end my life if I took a wrong step. In a way, I don't blame them— with a bleak outlook like that, there's hardly any room for understanding the abundant joy and comfort that I get from horses. Therefore, I was always trying to find a way to get a "horse fix". There was much wheedling and cajoling through my younger years, and once I had the opportunity, I started doing barn chores in exchange for riding time. Many professional equestrians got their start this way, so I figured it was a matter of time before my dedication and determination led me towards superstardom.

But then something happened that changed the course of my history: I attended my first horse show as a rider. I had been to loads of horse shows before, in the capacity of a groom/assistant/runner/barn hand, and I had the time of my life. There was always something going on. I spent the day dashing from ring to ring to make sure riders had all the supplies they needed, keeping horses and humans fed and hydrated, and keeping all of our equipment accounted for and hopefully in the right place.

Riding in a show was different. After you warm up, it's a lot of standing around waiting for your class or round to be called. The weather is invariably too hot or too cold for what you're wearing, so you spend the day shivering in clothing that's only practical for the show ring, or drenched in sweat, gasping for air. The restroom is always at the furthest point from the ring in which your classes are being called, and the chaos that is so charming from the ground– a cacophony of eager and anxious people, horses, and dogs with very different agendas– becomes a safety hazard.

Despite the fact that I placed well in my classes, I didn't find horse shows fun. Hunter/jumper riding had more or less been foisted upon me through collaboration between my father and my riding instructor when I was just seven years old. My father thought the outfits were nice and boring– black jackets and beige breeches with tall black leather boots– and my instructor thought I had the right level of precision and perfectionism to make it around the ring with finesse. While I thought I had been having a good time, maybe I was simply in the wrong sport.

So I hopped in every saddle that was offered to me for several years. I learned a thing or two about reining. I hung out with some competitive trail riders. I took lessons with a show jumper and learned about tight spaces and fast paces. Western pleasure. Gaited horses. Then, one day I found myself in a very dark barn– lit by just two arena floodlights– with a very large 18-hand gray horse, having my very first dressage lesson. It all clicked- This was what I wanted to do with my life.

Dressage has been compared to dancing with a horse, and from the ground, it looks like the horse and rider are performing lovely, floating steps. In the saddle, however, it's a matter of relaxing your body and brain while simultaneously using every named part of your body and flowing both with and against the motion of the horse to create shapes, paces, and movements. Dancing is a fair assessment, but I'd be more inclined to call it yoga.

At the same time, I'm still not moved by the spirit of competition. I rode in dressage shows throughout my intercollegiate career and continued competing in hunter/jumper shows as well. But, I was bored. My ribbons resided at my parents' houses. I skipped the regional shows I qualified for because I didn't want to go. My college coach– who is still my mentor to this day– didn't push me to go because she understood. Sometimes it's not about the shows.

Instead, I wanted to have fun. I wanted to have the most fun possible, in the safest possible way, with horses I truly understood. And that right there is enough work to keep me busy every day.

There's nothing wrong with showing. Many of my horsey friends thrive on regular trips into the show pen. It is thrilling to hear your name called over the loudspeaker, watch your points accumulate, get end-of-the-year awards and prizes, and have measurable improvement in your riding and career.

There's also nothing wrong with not showing, or showing rarely. There's nothing wrong with barrel racing in an English saddle if you feel like it, or riding with no saddle at all. In fact, you can own a horse for its entire life and never ride it once, and that's perfectly fine. While there's a lot of pressure in the horse world to be the best in the world, I don't agree with that philosophy.

I believe, as do many equestrians, that the top consideration of horse ownership should be the partnership you build. I've noticed a sad decline in the number of people who truly bond with and understand their horses. When I started giving lessons years ago, I would ask riders who had owned or been working with their horses for months or years what their horses liked. What was their personality? What did they enjoy? They couldn't tell me. "He likes food, I guess?" "He likes it when I take him outside to eat grass." "She likes winning ribbons."

While I don't like coming off as preachy, I do feel it's very important to know your horse in a real way. My first horse hated peppermints. Maxwell hated hugs. Dolly liked it when I gave her scratches right above her tail. Red has two specific two very specific favorite brushes. Belle thinks zippers are the best invention ever. Just like any living being, horses have preferences and patterns in their lives. When you share your life with one of these animals, it's your responsibility to learn what makes them happy.

At the same time, you don't have to stand there and stare at your horse to receive that information. Interacting with your horses in a meaningful way will tell you much more about their personality than watching what the critter does of his own volition. Therefore, I encourage every horse owner to work with their horses. You ask, "Now what?" I say, "Work with your horse."

In this book, we'll look at all of the different meanings of that phrase. "Work" doesn't mean you have to plow the fields, jump a 5-foot fence, or start schooling canter pirouettes… but you can if you want to. It is my goal to empower horse people of every level of experience and understanding to learn how to spend meaningful time with their horses.

We'll start with the basis for it all: groundwork. Being able to control and understand your horse while you both have your feet on the ground is the foundation from which everything you do behind the reins is built. Furthermore, groundwork establishes boundaries, safety, and confidence.

Then, we'll take a look at a variety of different equine sports. Whether you choose to dip your toes in the basics or head full steam into a competitive lifestyle is up to you and your horses. We'll look at what the sport entails, the type of training and movement required, the equipment needed, and what type of professional can help you get to the level where you and your horse feel most comfortable. It's a lot to cover, so consider this an introduction to your new favorite sport rather than a comprehensive guide to doing absolutely anything with a horse.

Lastly, I'll provide you with a few insights into getting into the horse community. As always, there will be a "Resources" section to help you network, research, and learn more about equine events in your area, or in general. As I mentioned in my first book, learning should be a constant for those who aspire to have long, happy, and healthy relationships with their horses.

You have a horse… now what? Now you start having the most amazing time of your life with your new big, stinky, and fuzzy buddy.

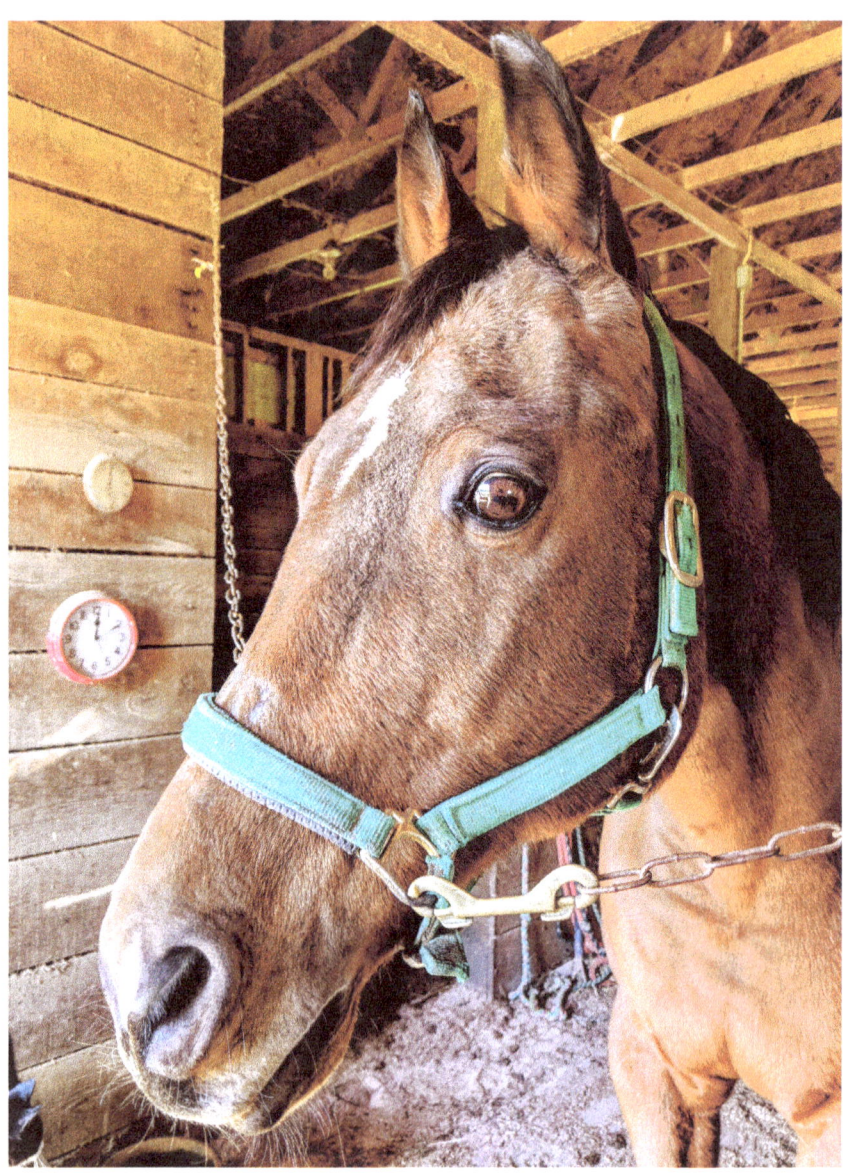

PART 1: GETTING TO KNOW YOUR HORSE

How do you "get to know" a horse? Do you walk into its stall and say, "Hi, horsey. My name is (your name). I'm going to call you (horse's name). How do you do?"

You might laugh, but it's not a half bad idea.

Early in my equine career, I had an instructor who forbade us from talking to the horses. "They don't understand what you're saying, and you're not allowed to use voice cues when you show, anyway." Fair points, but since this particular trainer, I've not met a single person who *doesn't* talk to their horse.

Maybe your horse doesn't understand your full introduction, but horses, like any animal, can learn to recognize a variety of cues, whether spoken or unspoken. Horses, in particular, are keen on picking up specific motions, words, and the tone of your voice. Belle, for example, has been trained to respond to a variety of clicks, smoochy noises, and hums to perform various gaits. Racehorses are trained to urinate when you whistle. While a horse may not have an appreciative understanding of *Hamlet's* "To be or not to be" soliloquy, he can be trained to recognize a variety of words and sounds.

Furthermore, something interesting happens when we speak out loud around our horse: we act like ourselves. Our observant horses pick up on our tones and our moods and respond. I have seen many professionals use harsh tones of voice to get a horse to knock off naughty behavior, while I have seen a soothing voice help calm a nervous horse. Often, the way we speak and act align closely, and your horse will respond to tension, anger, sadness, nervousness, and calmness accordingly.

Therefore, my first recommendation is to talk to your horse. Tell it what you want it to do. Share with it how you're feeling. Explain what you're going to do during your time together in a particular session. Ask why it has a particular bad habit, or keeps doing something annoying. That early instructor was right in that they aren't going to participate in conversational English dialogue, but they will respond. They'll respond to key words they know, and they'll learn about your moods and actions.

However, don't make the conversation one-sided. Listen to your horse, too. Horses have a lot to say. Whether it's throwing their head as high in the air as they can to signal discomfort, or sticking out their bottom lip when you find a good scratchy spot, horses are constantly communicating. Think about how they talk to each other too. Horses mainly speak to each other with body language. They bump into, nibble on, kick at, rear at, dart away from, and lick each other to share their preferences with their herdmates. And just as you communicate with them in the language you know, they'll "talk" to you in their language as well.

So, getting to know your horse is a matter of learning how to talk to each other, even though you don't speak the same language. That doesn't mean you should stop speaking your own language— you just need to spend some quality time together so you can each learn what each other's sound or gesture means.

And that, in a nutshell, is the foundation for every great human-equine relationship. Let's get started on learning the basics of communication between horse and human.

SECTION 1: SALUTATIONS AND GREETINGS

Have you ever watched two horses meet each other for the first time? It can be pretty dramatic, depending on the characters involved.

Typically, it starts with sniffing. Nostrils flared to process as much of each other's scent as possible, they breathe loudly, assessing each other with arched necks. If a threat is imminent, that arched neck position will allow them to retreat quickly, or lash out with teeth bared, depending on whether flight or fight is more appropriate.

There will be some snapping, grunting, squealing, and a noise I can only describe as "honking". They may strike at each other with their front hooves, or turn their hindquarters and kick into the other's face. As a human standing on the ground, it can be more than a little disconcerting. Horses can be brutal to each other in their introductions, but that's part of establishing their roles in the herd.

Some horsemanship experts feel that your horse should see you as the "head of the herd." You should be the alpha, and your horse should submit to you. I don't entirely like the way that sounds, though I think I know what these experts are trying to impart. Your horse should understand not to snap at you, strike at you with his hooves, or act like a general fool when you appear. However, there's no reason for your presence to be intimidating to your horse.

In this section, I'll share some tips for meeting your horse on common ground. I don't claim to be a horsemanship expert, but as someone who has worked with horses around the country for over thirty years, I admit I have a fair amount of experience with the topic of creating a decent working relationship with horses I have never met before. I'm not going to solve all of your problems, but I intend to give you some hope and understanding.

I also encourage you to work with a professional, especially if this is your very first horse, or you're new to horses in general. Working with a rank horse can be very dangerous, and I recommend having a buddy around in case of an emergency. If your horse is asking you questions you cannot answer, it is appropriate and strongly encouraged to enlist the help of someone with more experience on the matter.

I recommend starting slowly when meeting your new horse for the first time, so let's take it step-by-step from saying "hello" to learning how to speak the same language fluently.

Chapter 1: An Introduction to Introductions

First impressions are everything. When you meet someone for the first time, the way each of you behave and interact will become a lasting memory.

This is actually true regardless of the species involved in the interaction. We've all seen dogs sniff each other's derriére, or cats spit and wave at each other. When a horse meets a new horse, they sniff each other's faces, paw at the ground, squeal, and even nip a little to help them understand their relationship to one another. Sometimes equine relationship building involves more physical interaction with running, fighting, and kicking used as measures to demonstrate dominance and tolerance.

Obviously, as smaller, far more fragile beings, we want to avoid getting in a kick-fight with a larger, incredibly powerful horse. Therefore, the way you approach your new horse really matters, especially as you're starting to get to know each other.

For the first few months of your new partnership, I recommend exercising caution around your horse. Be on high alert because your horse will likely be as well. As a prey animal in a new place, he likely has no idea what's really going on. He woke up, ate breakfast, walked into a box, the box started moving, and now he's here. Unless your new horse is an experienced show horse who has been dragged all over creation and is used to waking up in new barns, this is going to take some getting used to.

My first recommendation is to let the horse smell you. Every time you approach him, let him sniff your outstretched hands. Some horses will try to get into your face as they would with another horse, but as a human, you have the right to decide if you will permit this behavior or not. Some people strictly enforce a barrier around their person that the horse cannot enter. Similarly, some horses have no interest in entering your personal space anyway.

Others, myself included, allow horses to touch them once they've established a few basic rules, namely: no teeth. Horses communicate a lot with their teeth since they can't use their hands or fingers to gesture like humans do. Different nips mean different things and can actually be a sign of affection in some cases. Unfortunately, humans have very thin skin compared to horses and even the most loving bites hurt us. Therefore, do not encourage a horse to nip at you. Should your horse start to explore your coat, hat, or glasses with his mouth, a gentle flat hand pop to the nose and a "NO BITE" command should do the trick. If it doesn't, you might have a biter on your hands. That means no hand feeding treats and dodging that mouth until it learns to stay shut. In extreme cases, you may wish to work with a professional behavioralist to help your horse unlearn this vice.

So, here you are in front of your new horse, who has sniffed you completely. Now what? This is where you interact with your equine companion. Talk to him. Stroke his neck and face and move around his body, but be sure to keep an eye on the horse's body language as you do so. Ears upright and swiveling mean he's paying attention and listening– that's a good sign. Ears turned backwards and slightly horizontal mean he's not entirely happy with what you're doing, but willing to entertain your thoughts unless they escalate. Ears plastered to the head completely are a sign to stay away.

Just as some humans have a strictly enforced personal space, so do many horses, at least until they get to know you. If you've only worked with lesson horses or horses that deal with a lot of people on a regular basis, they'll probably have more relaxed rules about who can touch them and where. This part might be over quickly as they learn to recognize you as a "regular human," who will interact with them on a daily basis. Horses might be one of the more reactive creatures on this planet, but they're definitely not without intelligence!

Therefore, don't be surprised at how much or how little time it takes for your horse to accept you into his personal space. Don't be shocked if he spooks when you drop a brush, or if he turns his hindquarters to you and becomes offended when you walk into his stall to clean it. Horses love routine, so it may take your new buddy some time to learn the ins and outs of his new home.

You can make this easier for him by greeting him each time you go out to the barn. I actually hollar, "Good morning, Ponies!" to the herd I care for each time I come out to feed. Some of them even greet me in return. As I mentioned earlier, I'm a strong believer in talking to horses. Not only does it set the mood, but it helps you maintain clarity and focus when working with your horse. Best case scenario? Your horse learns the sound of your voice and your body language.

Worst case scenario? Your horse tunes you out and daydreams about carrots and green pasture as far as the eye can see. As far as I can tell, it's not really much of a loss!

Chapter 2 : Reach out and Touch Your Horse

Another great way to bond with your new horse is through the act of grooming. There are so many schools of thought on the necessity of and proper technique for grooming that I can hardly cover it all here. However, since this can be a fantastic way for you and your horse to get to know each other, I'm going to include the basics.

Personally, I see grooming as a great opportunity to check up on your horse. As you brush them from head to hoof, you can check them over for any interesting heat, swelling, or abrasions. Horses can be shockingly clumsy, even within the confines of a stall. In fact, you might notice that a horse who rarely leaves his stall has swollen legs. Known commonly as "stocking up," this swelling is a harmless accumulation of blood and other fluids. In most cases, letting your horse walk around will help the swelling go down.

But, regular grooming of your horse will help you learn the differences between something simple, such as stocking up, versus a real problem. Swelling and heat can be signs of all sorts of trouble, from an abscess in the hoof to a puncture wound or tendon injury. Knowing your horse's topography can help you know when to call the vet and when to cold hose and hand walk your companion.

Additionally, brushing your horse can help keep his coat healthy, although some experts disagree on how frequently or with how much vigor you should brush your horse. Here are my basic thoughts on grooming:

- A daily once-over– including a basic dust off and hoof pick– is good for catching problems or injuries before they become a big deal. If you're going to be working with your horse, make sure there isn't any dirt, burrs, or other debris in the areas where you and the tack will come in contact with the horse's body. Just as you wouldn't want to run laps with a pinecone in your pants, your horse prefers not to chafe while he works too.
- If your horse is covered in mud or dirt, clean it off. While it's true that wild horses run around muddy with no problem, your domesticated horse needs to be able to fluff his coat when it's cold, sweat when it's hot, and slick the water off of his skin when it's raining.
- A regular, thorough brushing can help keep skin healthy. "Regular" can mean many things, though. Red has a history of skin fungus, so he gets a thorough grooming far more often than Belle, who has never had problems.
- If you live in a climate where your horse grows and sheds a thick, shaggy winter coat, help relieve him of that extra fluff when temperatures warm up. Yes, he'll shed naturally, but if you're planning on increasing his workload, remember that he's wearing his winter coat while he works. He'll sweat more and become tired more easily, just as you would if you wore a snow suit in warmer temperatures. Clipping a horse's sweatiest areas can be very helpful for preventing overheating or getting a chill from being too wet.
- Shampooing and conditioning a horse's mane, tail, or body isn't something you need to do frequently unless you are going to be hitting the shows, or your horse has skin/hair issues that you're addressing. Horses produce oils naturally that help keep their skin and hair healthy, so while it might be helpful to fully wash an exceptionally muddy or sweaty horse, you don't need to worry about throwing your horse in the bathtub every night. In fact, please don't– it would probably break the porcelain.

Do I really groom my horse every single day? Most of the time, no. When the weather is warm and their coats are short, it's much easier to check them for flesh wounds. Plus, both of my horses are actively working in my trainer's lesson program, which means my trainer and keen students are also grooming and interacting with them daily.

One of the most important things about the act of grooming is that it can be some of the best bonding time between a horse and a human. You're both relaxed and sharing space together. You can take this time to understand what kind of touching your horse enjoys, and which he despises. Red, for example, loves this thin rubber nubby grooming glove I have and hates regular curry combs. If you rubbed his face with it all day, it might not be long enough for him. Belle, on the other hand, likes really stiff body brushes and will lean her shoulders into a nice hard brushstroke. They're all different, and the only way to really find these connections is through jumping in and trying various brushes and techniques.

I encourage any first time horse owner to get a variety of brushes, including a curry comb, stiff body brush, soft face brush, and hoof pick with a brush on the end of it. Personally, I like to pick out my brushes in person, so I can see how each tool feels in my hands. For example, bigger brushes can be harder to grip for people with smaller hands. You don't need to buy the super-expensive brushes at first, unless you really want to and your budget permits. Look for something that will stand up to heavy fur and mud removal, but expect that at some point, it will be dropped in manure, stepped on, and eventually lost in the darkest corners of your tack trunk or brush bins.

Over time, you'll discover that you've accumulated an uncanny number of your horse's favorite brushes, which will all look ratty and gross compared to the versions your horse doesn't like as much. As you take stock of your brushes, you'll likely call up certain memories associated with each one. Like the time you dropped that blue brush under your horse, and you weren't sure how best to retrieve it. Or the time your horse came in super muddy, and you were so glad you had that one green scrubby thing.

These memories will serve as your proof that the time spent fussing over your horse's hair and hooves hasn't been time spent in vain. You've learned a lot about your horse in that time. You should be familiar with your horse's body and the way he acts when you brush here or scritchy-scratch there. Or how his lower lip sticks out when you brush right there, and he stubbornly refuses to pick up that hoof on the first try. That's getting to know your horse. That's building a relationship. And it's all right there, at the end of the brush.

Chapter 3 : Building Friendship through Groundwork

The word "groundwork" is flung around in the equestrian community like an old rag. Everyone who has been around horses for more than a few years has their own version of groundwork that they will swear is the one and only way to work with a horse. While that's definitely not true, these so-called experts aren't exactly wrong, either.

You see, groundwork is really just communication exercises between humans and horses. As you look around and think of all the humans you interact with on a daily basis, you'll realize that everyone has a different communication style. For example, some might speak too loudly, and others might speak too softly. Some people might have a tone that comes across as sharp and bossy, while others seem dismissive and uninterested in the conversation. Some people speak very quickly, while others speak very slowly.

In fact, you might find that you have to work harder to understand some of your acquaintances than others. You might have to ask the fast talkers or low talkers to repeat themselves. You might get impatient and angry when the slow talkers take their time getting to the point. While horses don't speak a human language, they have a fine-tuned ability to learn body language, tone of voice, and some verbal commands. However, just as you might have no idea what your human friend says when they mumble, your horse might not have any clue what you're trying to impart upon him at first. You need to learn how to communicate with each other, hence the groundwork.

My personal thought is that each horse needs to know at least a few basic ground manners. I need to be sure that whatever horse I'm leading from his stall to the pasture is going to walk politely next to me. When I need him to stop, he will stop. When I remove the lead rope from his halter, I need him to wait politely for me to step away before he takes off. If I drop the lead rope for any reason, I need him to stand still and wait for me to pick the rope back up.

However, groundwork can go far beyond that. I've taught Red how to shake hands, and he'll follow me around an obstacle course without a halter or lead rope. Belle can spin, side step, back up, and follow me based on my body position. Both of my horses free lunge without a rope, and they switch between gaits based on voice commands and hand gestures. People do all sorts of "tricks" with their horses, but at the end of the day, they're establishing and fine-tuning their communication with each other.

There are many experts out there who would be thrilled for you to invest your time and money into their training programs. If you choose to go this route, I highly recommend that you take the time to investigate the trainer. Don't just watch a few videos, but Google the trainer's name to see what kind of reputation they have as a human. Put yourself in your horse's steel bar shoes— consider how you would feel applying the trainer's techniques on yourself. Horses aren't at the same cognitive position as humans, but if what the trainer is doing offends you, then chances are it will also annoy your horse.

Most groundwork experts can, however, agree on some of the basics. For example, if you are leading your horse with a rope attached to his halter, he should be cheerfully moving at a similar pace with his head aligned with your right shoulder. When you stop, he should stop. When you start walking again and ask him to move forward, he should do so. So, what do you do if your horse doesn't have these magical command buttons?

In many instances, your horse will follow you out of curiosity or anticipation of where you might be going. If your horse has a specific routine such as going out to their field after breakfast, they'll probably be inclined to follow along very politely because they know where they're going and why. But as a human who is much smaller and slower than a horse, you want them to follow along politely even if they have no idea where they're going. If you discover that your horse doesn't want to leave the barn through a specific door or leading your horse becomes a battle of wills, you might want to revisit basic groundwork.

Start small. As in, start in a small area where if your horse gets loose, it's not going to be a big problem. An arena, round pen, or smaller paddock is ideal for groundwork because you can allow your horse to make choices about his movement without risking him deciding he's done and running off into the sunset.

I recommend taking every safety precaution you can as well. Wear thick leather gloves if you're going to be doing work with a lead rope or lunge line. Choose ropes that are comfortable in your hands, and not too light and thin or too heavy and bulky. A helmet can protect your head in case things get weird. Establish an escape route. Wear appropriate footwear– absolutely no sandals.

Also, be prepared to let go. Our number one reaction when working with a bolting horse is to hang on. This is bad because in most cases, horses have no problem dragging your body weight behind them as their adrenaline-filled brains urge them to gallop far away from what frightens them. While letting go might not be ideal when a small pen or arena is not available, it is much safer than your terrified, frantic horse dragging you on your face at top speed.

Start slow as well. Take just a few steps at a time. When reinforcing a horse's ability to lead politely, attach the lead rope to his halter. Walk forward a few steps and ask him to walk alongside you. Then stop. When you stop, your horse should stop. Walk five steps, then stop again. Stand still. Make your horse wait for you to urge him to move forward again. Walk ten steps and repeat the exercise. Vary the number of steps you take at a time and how long you wait before walking off again.

If your horse has been trained well, a quick refresher with his new human should be enough to remind him what good manners are and the difference between "stop", "wait", and "go". If your horse is particularly excited by his new surroundings, you might need to repeat yourself a few times. And if your horse has never been taught good manners, you'll be starting from scratch.

If he's tossing his head around, jogging in place, trying to go up, down, or sideways, or trying to dash off, you might want to put a chain over his nose. The point of the chain isn't to hurt the horse, but rather, to create pressure he can't ignore. Remember– you're small and a different species. You need to be able to command your horse in a way he will recognize. Since horses use teeth, hooves, and loud noises to get each other's attention, you need to step up your game from muttering curse words and pulling, since these are very ignorable when you're 1,200 pounds and desperately interested in what your buddy is doing in that field over there. You should be able to give the chain a quick tug from the ground to get your horse's attention. If you leave a mark, you're using far too much pressure.

Likewise, if your horse balks and refuses to move forward, you might want to bring a long lunge whip along to encourage the back end of your horse to go forward without putting yourself directly behind the horse. Again, you're not trying to cause the horse pain, but create a sense of pressure that he'll want to move away from.

Remember that at the very core of their being, horses are prey animals. Their first instinct is to remove themselves from the vicinity of intimidating things. The end of the whip, though logically not frightening, mimics scary things in nature just closely enough that your horse is hard-wired to respect it, even if he doesn't yet respect you. The whip is also much longer than our human arm span, which means you don't have to be close to the horse's danger zones when you use this tool.

The goal of any tools you use when schooling groundwork is not to be mean or violent, but to be safe. You want your horse's attention on you so that he doesn't accidentally run you over, step on you, or bolt off taking your arm and shoulder with him. Leading horses with bad ground manners is a very prominent cause for human injury, especially those to the hand, wrist, or shoulder. Nearly every equestrian over a certain age has lost full range of motion of their neck and shoulders, and as someone who fits in that category, I encourage you to avoid injury. No horse is 100% predictable, but a horse with good manners is more likely to react to scary situations more appropriately.

Over time, your horse may be willing to follow you without a lead rope, stopping, walking, jogging, and doing patterns based only on your cues. Bear in mind, however, this won't happen immediately. Many new equestrians become very frustrated when they start working with an unfamiliar horse because it can take months or even years to develop a truly harmonious bond with a horse. Continue to put in the work, repeat the exercises, and be patient– you are learning to speak a language that neither of you have spoken before.

In fact, the "Stop/Go" exercise I've just outlined is an exercise you'll want to repeat frequently, until you and your horse are on the same page. Every time I work with any horse, I do a quick check on where their brains are by walking a few steps, stopping, waiting, and walking off again to see how quickly and completely they respond to my cues. Even though I'm on the ground next to them, their reaction to these simple commands lets me know what has their attention and whether they're feeling peppy, sluggish, or are completely focused on me.

This is, of course, just one of the many types of groundwork exercises you can practice with your horse, but one that I feel is at the foundation of every relationship between a human and a horse, no matter how short or temporary. As someone who has worked with many horses in many situations, I cannot stress enough the importance of feeling confident when leading a horse, even if it's just a few steps. The more you practice groundwork, the more capable you'll feel, regardless of whether you're working with your trusty steed of dozens of years, or a new beast who has just come off the trailer. And as for the horse, he'll be pleased to know who's in charge around here and to whom he should address his attention.

Chapter 4 : What If My Horse Doesn't Like Me?

It's actually somewhat concerning how often I hear people complain that their horse "doesn't like them." Or, if I'm speaking with someone who has limited contact with horses, they might whine, "Horses just don't like me."

Some horses don't like people. Some horses don't like certain people. But if your own personal horse doesn't like you, you really shouldn't gloss over that fact. And if all horses universally dislike you, perhaps you should address the common denominator.

Nearly every undesirable equine behavior traces back to the fact that they are prey animals. They are naturally highly reactive to things that trouble them. A lot of things trouble them. You should not be one of those things.

When people tell me their horse doesn't like them, I ask them if they like their horse. It's a harsh question, but a very serious one as well. If you don't bond with your horse through simple activities such as grooming and groundwork, it is far more likely that you two will not develop a great relationship. Sometimes, that is not anyone's fault. I have known several horses that simply wanted nothing to do with me— either because they were bonded to another person, or because they had been in an environment that led them to not trust any human. However, in most cases, spending a significant amount of time with your horse will at the very least help you establish a working relationship.

The concept of "joining up" has changed faces several times within my three decades of working with horses. When I was a young equestrian, I was encouraged to spend time with my horses outside of working with them. I'd see other riders eating a sandwich outside their horse's stall, standing outside their horse's stall and idly stroking his face while chatting with barn friends, and sitting on a stool reading a horse magazine to figure out their next training ride— essentially, we were encouraged to just hang out with our horses.

Then came the "Horse Whisperers" of the 1990s, and suddenly there were several different theories of what "joining up" meant and how to achieve it. Some believe it means making your horse move his feet and body towards his human, while others insist your horse should move away from pressure. Some equine behaviorists think the horse should see you as herd leader, while others feel horses gain confidence by exploring on their own.

So, who's right? In my experience of attending dozens of clinics and working with many different experts, everyone has valid points. I personally train my horses to move towards me **and** away from me, based on different cues. I want my horses to follow me around, but I don't want them so dependent on me that they are incapable of thinking when I'm not there to tell them what to do.

My own personal "joining up" exercise combines a lot of these ideas. I do hang out with my horses each day. I talk to them and interact with them, or stand by their stall and give them scritchy scratches on their ears while I talk to my trainer. I see no reason not to do this. But when I work with them, I occasionally take them off the lead in the arena to see what happens.

Bear in mind, I only do this with horses who have manners, and who I trust will not immediately run me over when we're sharing a space. I'd recommend being solid on "Stop/Go" commands before sharing a small area with any horse at liberty.

You might be wondering what to expect to happen, and honestly, it depends on how your horse is feeling that day. Red is especially trustworthy at liberty, and some days, he'll wander around the arena and sniff things while I do chores. Sometimes he'll roll in the dirt, bounce back to his feet and gallop around until his inner "yeehaw" has been expressed. Other times, he follows me around, casually observing my weird two-legged behaviors. When I'm done, I give him the command to come back (if he's not already lurking behind me or waiting patiently at the gate for me), and we head back to his stall.

What do we get out of this? Today, it mainly reaffirms our trust for each other. I am confident that he's not going to do anything harmful or inappropriate, and he knows his boundaries and when to listen to me.

When we were first introduced, he would spend a lot of his time hanging out in the corner of the arena, ignoring me. I'd walk over to greet him, and he'd swivel his ears. Sometimes he'd let me approach, and other times he told me to back off. Other times, he would abruptly pivot and gallop off in the other direction.

The point of the exercise isn't necessarily to always catch the horse or have the horse come on command. Instead, it's about learning to communicate. Let's look at it as if both parties were human, but spoke different languages. Say, for example, you speak Dutch, but your coworker speaks Spanish. It would be as if your goal is to learn how to communicate with each other in fluent Korean. Think about how you would go about such a task. There would be a lot of gesturing and communicating through body language. You'd make a lot of mistakes and so would your coworker. You would both get frustrated with the task. And most of all, you would expect it to take some time.

Before you start asking a horse to respond to your complex commands in a work environment, you should understand how to communicate in the first place. Sometimes behavior that is described as "naughty" is just a misunderstanding. In the dressage world, for example, upper level horses are cued for a canter with the inside leg, while lower level horses or horses that do not exclusively compete in dressage use a cue from the leg by the wall. Riders who are accustomed to horses trained to spur stop will be in for a surprise when they get more forward action from a horse who is trained the other way around. Without knowing a horse's particular language, you could be confusing the horse for a very long time before you realize you're simply asking the question in a language he doesn't understand.

The concept of "joining up," in all of its various formats and definitions, nearly always boils down to getting to a point where you and your horse understand each other. Once you have the ability to understand each other, you have unlocked the potential to build a relationship.

Does this mean your horse is going to love you, fawn over you, and neigh joyfully every time you enter the barn? No. There may still be days when you flat out don't like each other. But, there are probably days when you don't like your boss, brother, or next-door neighbor too.

We all have moods, opinions, ideas, and preferences. Some people feel you should train your horse so that he is unable to express any of those. I've met horses like that and understand the means used to create that behavior, but I personally do not advocate it. Instead— however New Age or suspicious this might seem— I think it's much more meaningful to learn how to communicate with your horse so that he is able to collaborate with you when you work together. In my opinion, a horse that reacts to danger is far safer than one who stands there and lets a disaster happen.

If you are under the impression that your horse doesn't like you, consider calling a truce and starting from the beginning. Get to know each other. Start back at the very beginning with regular grooming. Hang out together. Figure out what your horse likes, from treats to brushes to movements and more. Take the time to learn the language the two of you will be speaking for the rest of your lives together, and you might just find that your compatibility increases dramatically.

Author's Anecdote- Thawing the Ice Princess

The more I reflect, the more I realize there are several horses and ponies in my past who could be referred to as an "ice princess." Mares, in particular, are very hot-cold creatures. That is, they approve of what you're doing, or they despise you for existing. That's only slightly a hyperbole– I have known several riders and trainers who have refused to take on mares because of their perceived attitude.

I don't like to generalize, but I've found that when I'm experiencing a personality clash with a horse, that horse is female. Still, I have known several mares that I have loved deeply, including my very own Belle, who perhaps reigns supreme over all "ice princesses." Not only was she cold when I acquired her– she was completely frozen.

I met Belle many years ago when she was fresh from her first 60 days of training. My friend bought her as green broke, mainly for her bloodline. If Belle didn't excel in any equine sport, my friend was confident that she would at least be a good investment as a broodmare.

The trainer came, and I started noticing that she spent very little time working with Belle. Soon, it came to light that the trainer was afraid of riding Belle because when she made the horse mad, she would spook. Belle is pretty smart, so she just started acting like a fool when the trainer tried to work with her which scared her off. Since the trainer needed money, she lied to the owner about what she was doing and hadn't trained her a bit.

Belle's owner fired the trainer and took her to a small, quiet barn, where she calmly, slowly, and quietly worked with her one-on-one until the mare got her brain back. They competed at several shows and did very well. This is where I bow out of the story temporarily, as I began working with a new trainer and a new herd of horses. In fact, I more or less forgot about her until one day she showed up at my trainer's barn as a new lesson horse.

She was skinny and limping and plastered herself against the back wall of her stall for a few days. She was terrified of every creak and groan in the barn and snapped at people who entered her stall. Clearly, something had gone awry in the past several years. Even more obvious was the fact that Belle wasn't going to be used as a lesson horse any time soon.

Since I had worked with rescue horses, I was nominated to see if we could get Belle to come out of her shell. Motivated by my rage at whoever had gotten her to this state, I agreed.

The Stop/Go exercise was absolutely perfect. She was trained for horsemanship (which we'll explore in a bit), so she knew how to stop, wait, walk, ground tie, and do 180- and 360-degree turns on her hindquarters. But if I attempted to touch her, she would stop abruptly. Her body would freeze in place, except for her lower left eyelid which would tremble violently. That was her sign that things were not okay.

So I started letting her go in the arena to see what she would do. I realize this is in direct conflict with what I recommended earlier, and for a brief moment, I honestly wondered what I would do if she refused to be collected once we had reached a good stopping point.

Mercifully, that wasn't the case. The first day we did this, she ran to the gate connecting the main row of stalls to the arena in our barn. I tried to approach her, and she took off in a hurry to the other side of the arena. So I took a seat on one of the stools used for mounting blocks, and let her explore the arena.

First came the chaos. She didn't understand why she was loose, but she didn't have any good ideas as to what she should be doing at the moment, and the only other living creature around was just sitting there. She sped around the arena in fear of the unknown.

Then she decided to check out her environment. She sniffed jump standards along the wall, poles on the ground, and manure left behind by an ill-mannered student (it is polite to pick up manure in shared areas when you're done with them!). Every few strides, she'd look over to me to see what was going on, and if I had any input. I didn't.

Eventually, I stood up. This caused a new wave of chaos and investigation. I moved, and that wasn't quite as concerning. I moved more and more, and it became less and less worrisome to Belle. After about twenty minutes, she decided she really didn't care if I belted out "YMCA" by the Village People complete with choreography. I was no longer considered a threat, but I wasn't quite trustworthy yet.

Meanwhile, in the barn, I started hanging out by her stall door after feeding her. Not in a looming, malicious way– I wanted her to know that I was going to be present, but not necessarily interacting. I sat on a tack trunk and sent work emails, or called someone and chatted so she could get a feel for casual speech. It wasn't really extra effort because I was doing what I would usually do, but I made it a point for her to notice me doing it. I did it not because I believed we could magically meld our souls together, but because I wanted her to know my baseline. If all a horse hears is someone screaming at them, they're going to assume that screaming is how humans communicate. They'll either become aggressive and "scream" back, or avoid all contact and freeze. I wanted Belle to get out of the habit of thinking that everyone was screaming at her, and that we could just "talk" politely.

According to my notes, it took about a year for her to stop with the eye twitching. I've heard many horse people say that it's harder to undo someone else's horrible training than to do it right the first time, and I agree. Belle is much more personable than she was when she first arrived, but there are still days when she tries to respond to pressure with her teeth. She's a polite and beloved lesson horse, but there are times she becomes overwhelmed with information and reacts with a small spook. We'll continue to work on these things for the rest of our days together, I'm sure.

I've worked with horses that spook, bolt, rear, buck, dance sideways, slam riders into the wall, and more. But the most terrifying reaction is none at all. You don't know what to prepare for because the next step after freezing is usually the equine equivalent of a psychotic break, all adrenaline and brain stem with no cognitive function.

Every time Belle gives me a little snuggle with her muzzle, or pops her head out of her stall window to say hi when she hears my car pull up, it reminds me that while not every horse and human bond is the same, it still has the chance to be a positive and inviting situation for both creatures.

SECTION 2 : DECIDING WHAT TO DO WITH YOUR HORSE

So, what are your plans for your horse?

For some people, the answer to this question is straightforward and immediate. "I plan to work up through the Pony Club levels." "I would like to be ready to ride a First Level dressage test by April." "I'm going to wait for her to finish growing, then send her to my trainer to get her started with reining."

Others of us really don't have long-term goals. I ended up buying Belle as a complete fluke, and I didn't really think about what we would do together after the paperwork was signed and the check cleared the bank. I just figured I'd continue working with her, and at some point, she would tell me what she enjoys doing, and what she would rather not do.

Still, in other cases, the answer is quite simple: If you've found yourself with a very senior horse, a companion-only horse, or a horse that for any reason is considered "pasture-sound" only, you don't really need to choose an occupation for your horse.

However, it is important that you come up with some plans for you and your horse so that you have a reason to spend time together. Your horse will likely get bored eating, roaming, and staring into the wind day after day. Likewise, you might find yourself mentally detaching from a horse that you don't actually interact with, which might lead you to question why you're pouring money into something you don't even play with.

You don't have to have a specific, detailed, or even well-thought out plan for what you and your horse are going to accomplish together, but you do need to have some basic idea of what you're going to do today, tomorrow, and even next week.

This section and the following section are intended to help you discover and understand what you and your horse could potentially accomplish together.

The following chapters will help you appreciate the scope of what you and your horse can do. Before you decide what activities you want to try, what type of training you want to invest in, and start shopping for an instructor, it's a good idea to get a general idea of what is within the realm of possibility. I encourage every horse person to try out as many equine disciplines and activities as they can, but at the same time, we all need to recognize what is and what isn't a good idea for long-term success.

Therefore, let's get started by arranging our hopes and dreams into a set of realistic goals and steps to take along the way.

Chapter 1: What Do You Want to Do?

What do *you* want to do in the equine world? This is actually a really big question because everything else hinges on the answer to this question.

Most people have a sort of "bucket list" for things they want to accomplish with horses. As a completely horse-obsessed teenager, I compiled the following list, which I titled in very large, all-capital letters "HORSE THINGS I NEED TO DO." The list is as follows:

- Own a horse
- Have a horse on my own property
- Jump a 3-foot course
- Gallop bareback
- Ride a gaited horse
- Try carriage driving
- Take reining lessons
- Ride a horse through the mountains
- Win a ribbon for riding a dressage test
- Ride in a parade
- Go on a cattle drive
- Train a green horse
- Take dressage lessons from a big name trainer
- Teach riding lessons
- Gain confidence
- Have fun

As a horse-crazed teenager, I had friends who were also horse-crazed teenagers. One friend had a list that was a little more specific. It's been many years, so I don't have her exact list memorized, but I remember sitting in the common room at our lesson barn thinking, "Am I doing this whole horse thing wrong?" Her goals were a lot more organized than mine:

Achievement	When
Qualify for State Finals on the local hunter/jumper circuit	This year
Intern at Hunterdon	Application due 1/1
Compete in Maclays*	All qualifying points by 8/31 1998
Compete in Medals**	All qualifying points by 8/31 1998
Olympics	2012

*This is the familiar name for the The National Horsemanship Championship for the ASPCA Alfred B. Maclay Trophy– the most prestigious competition for Junior hunter/jumper riders

** The nickname for the Dover Saddlery/USEF Hunter Seat Medal Final – another elite competition for Junior hunter/jumper riders

I share these two lists as fantastic examples of how different everyone's response can be when asked, "What do you want to do?" Even in my younger years, I wanted to try as many different things as possible. Meanwhile, my talented friend was working on the finer details of starting her professional career.

Unfortunately, I lost contact with my friend when she moved away, but I truly hope she was able to accomplish many of the things on her list. I've checked off most of my list, but I still have a couple things left to try.

I highly encourage you to write your own equine bucket list. When you do, be sure to look beyond the words on the page and consider what's between the lines.

Let's look at my list again. Only one of those goals is competition-related. That indicates that my passion wasn't in winning ribbons and gaining recognition, but exploring my skills and abilities when riding and working with horses. I didn't have a particular timeline. There's no white-knuckle discipline or sense of urgency. Just some cool stuff to do with horses before I lose the ability to work with them.

On the other hand, my friend had very specific goals and due dates to motivate her. From her list, she could actually plot exactly what horse shows she needed to enter in order to gain the correct amount of points to qualify for the next step in the process. As a result, she was incredibly focused in every interaction with her horse. She took multiple lessons a week, worked at the barn to help pay off board, and attended every relevant clinic she could to get both education and exposure among the horse community. Her goals were professional, while mine were recreational.

Your own goals are going to be personal to you and your current level of experience, and there are no wrong answers. Be honest with yourself – you might be shocked to discover that what you truly want out of your interactions with horses is a little different than what you had expected. For the longest time, I was convinced that I would be a professional rider and trainer. But I don't like going to horse shows, and I definitely lack the discipline to ride for hour after hour, day after day. I have the skill and talent to accomplish professional status, but I don't particularly want to put in the work.

Let your passion guide this list, not your well-rehearsed answers to questions about why you work with horses. Think about what you really want to do, not what you should do or what others expect you to do. You don't have to be the best equestrian in the whole wide world. Instead, try aiming to be the most *satisfied* equestrian in the whole wide world.

Take your time. You might even want to keep a journal on the topic, as you may find your interests and goals change over time. If you've never taken a jump, a three-foot course may sound pretty cool. But after you've held your breath in terror over a few crossrails, you might re-evaluate that particular goal.

Be honest, be completely passionate, and don't rush your decision-making process. However, bear in mind that identifying what you want to do with horses will dictate how and what you do with your horse for all of your remaining days together. And that can be an absolutely magical thing.

Chapter 2 : What Does Your Horse Want to Do?

Your horse is an important part of this equation as well. While we like to think we can "make" our horses do anything, the truth of the matter is that everything we do successfully with our horses is based on mutual agreement. This is why we work so hard to build that dynamic working relationship described in the last section.

You'll want to build on this relationship to keep it healthy; therefore, I recommend creating goals and ideas of concepts you would like to work on. You want every moment you spend with your horse to be enjoyable, and that means learning to ride, drive, or handle your horse correctly, so that you are aware of how to encourage the best performance out of you and your horse. This will help you build an even better relationship as you work together, but even more importantly, it's fantastic for both of you, physically. You'll both build muscles, balance, confidence, and skills that can be beneficial in other areas of your life as well. Additionally, having a "job" will help your horse maintain his sanity, as he has something to think about besides mischief-making and pestering his buddies.

Your horse cannot specifically tell you what he wants to do; however, you can look at his resume to see what he might apply for. In my book, *Finding Your First Horse : How to Buy a Horse without Losing Your Mind (or Money)*, we review the process of selecting a horse to do a certain job. If you have a very specific goal, such as competing in the Olympics or working with cattle, you can save yourself a lot of pain by choosing a horse who has natural aptitude in those areas. However, if you're more interested in having fun and trying different things, you'll likely find yourself with what we call an "all-arounder."

Your horse's breed might say a lot about their skills and talents. Thoroughbreds, for example, are generally bred for speed and agility. Quarter Horses, Paints, Pintos, Appaloosas, and other stock breeds value traits like sturdy conformation, quick-mindedness, and versatility.

Similarly, your horse's conformation might say a lot about the things that make them happy. The length of their legs compared to their body, the angle of their shoulder, the build of their hindquarters, and even the positioning of their neck to their back can contribute to how well-suited a horse is for a particular task.

That being said, most horses are perfectly comfortable performing at lower levels of nearly every equine sport. Always double-check with your vet to ensure that it is safe for your horse and to understand what limitations or risks they might encounter physically, but most horses have the potential to be quite versatile.

It's just that pesky thing where they have thoughts and opinions, and maybe they just don't want to do that job. Every once in a while, a horse will absolutely put a hoof down when it comes to trying certain things. The bravest horse I ever met, who competed successfully and cheerfully in CCI3 Star FEI Three Day Eventing competitions (just a step down from Olympic level competition) more or less refused to do anything but jump big scary things and move effortlessly through the complex movements of a high level dressage test, to the point where he would stop in his tracks and not budge if asked to do something he found ridiculous.

Your horse will make it very obvious if they do not enjoy the task you have put before them. If he trips over or runs through obstacles, he's not a jumper. If his fastest speed is a good-natured lope, he's not a contesting horse. If he can't bear to be in the general vicinity of a cow, he's not a cattle horse.

If you're not immediately certain what you want to do with your horse, take the time to try as many different sports and activities as possible. However, pay attention to your horse's reaction to each new thing you try. Do his ears perk up, steps seem lighter, and you feel that shift into performance mode when you do certain things? Or does he balk, throw it into reverse gear, and have a tantrum when you ask him to give something a whirl?

While it may seem dramatic to us as humans, either of these reactions are his way of telling you whether he enjoys a particular task or dreads it. A certain amount of persuasion may be required to get your horse to try new things in the first place. After all, they are very large prey animals who like to avoid confrontation and things that are difficult— but once that initial resistance is overcome, you'll get a very clear picture of whether your horse was born for this or doesn't ever need to try it again.

Chapter 3 : What Is Realistic for Both of You?

There are two very important words in the title of this chapter: "realistic" and "both."

When deciding what types of activities you'd like to explore with your horse, you need to consider the following words:

- Should
- Could
- Would

We know what your wants are as well as those of your horse. But now it's time to consider the reality of your situation. You'll want to find those magical crossroads where you and your horse can be happy working together regularly. Unfortunately, this means having to be honest with yourself in the face of your loftiest dreams.

I encourage you to consider this more as an exercise in looking for amazing opportunities than a chance to have your dreams squashed. You might find yourself drifting into the headspace of, "Well, since we can't do xyz…" but this is counter-productive. Instead of thinking of this as an exercise in what you *won't* be doing, consider it a positive way of understanding what you and your horse *can* accomplish together.

To keep honest to yourself and your horse's needs, ask yourself these questions:

- *What should my horse and I do together?* With this question, you are identifying what is physically possible for both of you. Horses and humans alike have limits as to what they can do. Not all humans can climb mountains without supplemental oxygen. Not all humans can do complex mental math. Not all humans can play concert piano. No matter how hard they try, the aptitude simply isn't there. However, many humans can hike up a hill, balance their bank account, and tap out "Chopsticks" on a keyboard. You and your horse may not be ideal candidates for the Olympics, but what if you make your goal a little less strenuous, and aim for ruling the world in the 2'3" Class?

- **What *could* my horse and I accomplish together?** This question builds off the last one. If we take Olympic qualification off the table, what are some opportunities that come into focus as very real possibilities? For those who enjoy the social aspect of the horsey world, perhaps you can join a local group that practices certain activities together, such as hunting, Gymkhana, or Trail riding. Maybe you can join a breed or sport organization that has state, regional, and world level showing that can provide you with endless goals both at home and in competition.

- **What would I be *willing to do* to make these goals happen?** This question is formatted a bit differently. It's an uncomfortable question, but extremely important to the equation of figuring out how you and your horse are going to proceed together. Dreams are wonderful, and you should nurture your dreams. However, dreams do not come true without a big scoop of hard work and humility. Whatever your goals are, you will be working towards them every time you work with your horse. Are you willing to make sacrifices in time and money so that you can reach your dreams? Are your goals important enough for you to prioritize them? Do you have the financial ability to invest in supplies, trainers, show fees, travel expenses, and so on?

As you read these questions, please remember— the occupation you choose for you and your horse doesn't have to be measured quantitatively. There's absolutely nothing wrong with saying, "My goal for my horse and I is to enjoy ourselves and always end our sessions together on a good note."

Furthermore, you'll want to recognize that every big goal has many little goals leading up to it. Your "big goal" might be to jump a three-foot course, but on the way to that goal, both you and your horse need to learn how to trot and canter over poles and become adept at jumping smaller fences first. Depending on where you and your horse are in your training and skill level when you meet, that three-foot course might be something you do the week you bring him home or a few years in the future.

It is very appropriate to ask yourself these questions frequently, especially if you are working with a young horse, or you are inexperienced. You may find that you have to pivot in your plans from time to time. Since learning is not linear, especially when both parties involved are autonomous beings, there will be setbacks. You will change your mind. Your horse will turn up lame, or you'll feel unwell.

Remember that the only standards to which you are accountable are your own. Your primary responsibility in working with your horse in any capacity is to the physical and mental well-being of both of you. Sure, it hurts when dreams don't come true, but there is a lot to be celebrated about recognizing when you've reached the top of your potential. Another horse might have the talent you need, or you might find that both of you excel in a completely surprising area of equine sports. There is no rush, and no need to push either the horse or yourself past your physical, mental, and emotional comfort zone.

Everyone wants to achieve certain goals with their horses, and that is both healthy and admirable. We all need to have an idea of what we want to do with our horses every day to keep us healthy and happy, even if that plan is as simple as just having fun together. I believe that maintaining physical and mental health of both parties should be the primary goal of any equine-human relationship.

I also believe that varies greatly between each equine and human. The goals I have for Belle are not the same as those for Red, just as my goals are not the same as many of my barn mates. What matters most, in my opinion, is that everyone is on the same page when it comes to accomplishing various feats, which can help your relationship with your horse become something you cherish for a very long time.

It might seem a little out of the realm of logic to emphasize the importance of the relationship between a horse and a human and take their feelings into consideration when it comes to choosing what you two accomplish together. However, my own opinion is that if you have the opportunity to build a good working relationship with your horse, why wouldn't you at least give it a try?

I find this especially true in the case of first-time horse owners. You have found yourself in an amazing situation, wherein you are able to connect and have a meaningful relationship with another sentient creature. Even if you never get on his back, you can enjoy each other's company. Even if he is a highly trained professional discouraged from snuggling random cute things, you and your horse can build mutual respect for each other.

It's not unrealistic to enjoy the presence of another living creature. We do it with dogs and cats all the time. We tend to view horses through a different lens since they are historically work animals. They're also very large and don't snuggle on sofas very well. But they are still very much living creatures, and if you choose to share your life and paycheck with one, why not enjoy every possible moment?

Author's Anecdote- Red's Very Specific List of Demands

I picked up Red when he was four years old. As of this writing, he is sixteen years old. It's fair to say we know each other very well.

When I first brought him home, my goal was to get him healthy enough to be ridden. Once it became apparent that he was going to be just fine, my goal was to canter him under saddle. He hadn't cantered for a rider since his days on the track, and no one was sure he even could. After he demonstrated he had a very nice canter, I came up with more long-term goals for our partnership.

I wanted to train him to jump a two-foot fence and perform a First Level dressage test. On the scale of difficulty in the general equine world, these are pretty basic requests. But at the end of the day, that's all I wanted to do, and that's all he should do, with his various health problems.

Moreover, Red demonstrated to me very early in our relationship that he wasn't super motivated to accomplish much. Instead of snapping to attention and doing groundwork with focus, he wanted to cuddle and play with the barn cats. He wandered off when anything cute and fuzzy walked by the arena like a dog, goat, or small child. We would have moments of work that were absolutely brilliant, but other days I would practically be begging him to go forward. The inconsistency in our work together was maddening.

So, why did I keep working with him? Because of his amazing calmness. Even as a racehorse fresh off the track, he demonstrated great mental capacity for problem solving. He's a big horse, and the barn at which we were boarding was pretty small. He often got tangled in things in the aisleway, and always stopped, carefully extracted himself, and went back to standing patiently.

Therefore, imagine my surprise when one day I arrived at the barn to a wild-eyed, rearing chestnut beast my barn owner described as "stark-raving mad." My snuggly Thoroughbred had blossomed into a large, equine-shaped ball of energy and emotion. I was concerned about his health, but I was also very worried that my mild-mannered horse had finally become the "brainless racehorse" stereotype overnight.

In my attempt to check him over in his stall, he shoved past me and took off at a dead gallop. I was absolutely petrified. Was he gone forever? Would he make it to the road and lose his footing? I cursed my extensive knowledge of equine behavior as every possible worst case scenario flooded my mind.

But, here's what actually happened: Red took off out of the barn. He ran the length of the pasture fence, which bordered the woods. He was angry about the tree branches poking him, so he bucked and galloped full out to get back out of the woods. He pranced around the parking lot for a bit, then found a patch of grass and started eating. I walked up to him, clipped the lead line to his halter, let him catch his breath, and it was just like nothing had happened.

Suddenly, it clicked : this was the utter essence of Red. Sure, he had occasional bursts of energy, but he didn't have the attitude to sustain it. A horse that competes needs to have the energy and determination to do well. If I took this horse to a show, we might have one amazing class, and then he'd be busy trying to snuggle with a pony. Red didn't want to go-go-go; he just wanted to have a little fun once in a while.

I took him to one show to prove this theory, and I was right on the money with my assessment. We plodded around the warm-up ring. Then he realized there were lots of strangers there and got excited. I took him in one class, where he stood at the fence and whinnied for most of it, followed by several very rapid, unbalanced canter circles. It was a Walk/Trot Equitation Class. There is no cantering in these classes, but there was also neither walk nor trot in my horse at that moment.

Once the class was over, he decided he wanted to hang out by the trailer and eat grass with his buddy. I tried tacking him up for another class, but he wasn't interested in listening to me. It just wasn't his gig, and since it's not mine either, I didn't see a reason to force the issue.

Now that the mystery of what my horse wanted to do was resolved, we started having more fun, which resulted in more productive work sessions. Sometimes I'd clip a lead rope on his halter, and we'd walk the trails on the property together. Sometimes I'd hop on bareback and just walk around. Other times, we'd pick up a particular skill, like lead changes, leg yield, or extended trot.

But most importantly, I learned what my buddy likes and doesn't like. He will not permit anyone to ride him in a place where he eats. That means no galloping across the pasture, or even doing pony rides in a paddock where he's been turned out before. He'll get very upset and bounce up and down if anyone tries to ride him in his play area. He will specifically tell me when he needs to be lunged before I ride, and when I can just hop on by pinning his ears at me and dancing in place when I try to get on. Sometimes, we'll be working on a particular skill, and he'll decide he needs to canter a few laps as a palette cleanser.

Likewise, I share my requests with him. When I say, "Pony Ride," he knows that I'm deep in my feelings or anxious, and that I just need him to plod around on a long rein while I gather myself. Once I'm ready to work, I'll pick up the contact on the reins, and he'll shift his gait into a more forward, ready-to-go stride.

I can happily say that every ride is a good ride because we can communicate. We have fights, but we're able to understand what the other is trying to "say" through their behavior. I'm willing to engage in more fights with him because we are able to work through them more easily than I can with a horse I don't know as well. We can find mutual ground, build into new skills, and have productive fights because we have worked together in the spirit of understanding.

PART 2 : AN INTRODUCTION TO EQUINE SPORTS AND ACTIVITIES

Many of you might have read the last section about goal-setting and thought, "Gee, that's great, but I'm not sure what I want to do." You might be new to horses, or you've never really considered dabbling in anything but your current sport.

Therefore, the second half of this book is dedicated towards helping you decide which sports and activities you and your horse may want to try. We'll take a look at various disciplines and the different types and styles of riding you can explore.

I want to mention that this is in no way to be considered a complete guide to everything horse-related. There are plenty of sports that don't regularly receive the attention they deserve, either because they are very niche— such as vaulting and circus trick riding— or overlap with other activities— for example, war reenactment riders. I don't want to diminish the skill and effort displayed by those equestrians because I admire all equine activities equally. However, I wanted to create a very basic outline of some of the most popular activities with the hopes that it will provide new equestrians with enough details to spark their interest to explore further.

To get the most out of this part of the book, I encourage you to read all of the sections first. Make a note of what intrigues you. Then head to the "Resources" section to find websites that will lead you to more information on each discipline.

For others, you may have a degree of certainty as to your path with your horse. You might be taking lessons with an instructor whom you admire greatly. You might think this part of the book has nothing to offer you. I still recommend you read this part of the book so you can gain greater insight into the vastness of the equestrian world. There may come a time when your interests or abilities change, or you might find yourself getting into a rut with your current training and need to find a little excitement. Just like humans, horses can get bored of doing the same thing over and over. Mixing things up once in a while can be very beneficial for helping you and your horse find new ways to problem solve and achieve results as a team.

As you read through the following sections, don't be afraid to think, "I'd like to try that." Even professional equestrians swap horses so they can learn new things about how horses move and perform. Therefore, without further ado, let's dive into some of the many exciting possibilities for equestrian enjoyment.

SECTION 1 : THE ENGLISH DISCIPLINES

There are two main types of saddles in the equestrian world: English, also known as hunt seat, and Western. "English" is so called because it directly descends from the manner of riding developed and popularized in England. The saddles were designed to provide mounted hunters and cavalry with an open seat, which would allow for flexibility and movement when galloping over fences and covering terrain that included hills, valleys, and streams.

In English riding, great emphasis is put upon the rider's position and effectiveness, known as "equitation". Their heels are down, their chest open, and their spine straight. But, appearances aren't everything. These disciplines involve a very specific and direct form of contact between the rider and the horse that requires a nuanced center of balance, a soft, following arm that connects directly with the horse's mouth via the bit, and an appearingly super-straight, tall spine. It's actually the result of fully activated abdominal muscles.

Hunt seat saddles are often very minimalist, especially jumping saddles. The panels are thin, the seats flat, and padding at the knees and thighs, known as "rolls" is for bridging the gap between the rider and horse's anatomy rather than providing comfort. The stirrups, known as irons, are connected to the saddle by thin stirrup leathers, which look impossibly thin and fragile. In truth, there's generally not a whole lot of equipment between the horse and rider.

Therefore, riders who are starting out with the English disciplines often feel very loose in the saddle and unstable. Developing a secure seat is the key to giving you a feeling of safety and helping you stay out of the horse's way when he moves.

However, it takes a lot of practice and confidence to feel secure. Many riders who switch to English disciplines after riding a different style for a while report feeling like their legs are swinging around wildly. Your first time in an English saddle, you might feel your spine try to curl into a comfortable fetal position. Your legs might grip the horse in terror, and your arms and shoulders may clench as you grip the reins in two white-knuckled hands.

You may feel so vulnerable and imperiled that you give up right then and there. Allow me to assure you that every single rider has felt completely insecure at some point in an English saddle.

I recall my first English lesson. I had been riding Western pleasure for a year, and it wasn't really my thing. I didn't dislike it, but I wanted to try this jumping thing, which meant changing saddles. My first ride in an English saddle was on the same horse I had ridden for my very first lesson years before. I had long since gained enough skill to ride other horses, but my instructor assured me I wanted to ride the easiest horse possible.

We never made it out of a walk. The minute my seat touched the unfamiliar saddle, my legs forgot where they were supposed to go. My heels shot up in the air. My hands couldn't figure out the short reins, and my neck immediately stiffened in fear, taking the rest of my body with it. I sat up there in solid fear until my instructor asked if we could please end the lesson early or switch to a Western saddle.
I did neither. My father moaned about spending money for me to walk around in

circles for an hour, but I was slowly gaining my balance. I was finding my place in the saddle and learning how to move my hips with the horse instead of bracing against the natural movement of his back. Soon, I was trotting, then cantering, and eventually, I was doing that jumping thing that had intrigued me in the first place.

Today, I like to share this story with my own students because I believe it's important to know that we all learn in different ways. For some people, sitting in an English saddle feels quite natural, especially if you have a stocky horse and a saddle that fits you well. But if you're a smaller person on a narrow horse or in a saddle that doesn't fit you well, you may feel wildly insecure.

As you read the following descriptions of some popular hunt seat disciplines, I want you to keep in mind that there are different levels of all of these sports. Everyone starts over ground poles before they go over fences. Everyone learns how to halt and salute at X before they do canter pirouettes. Being a beginner equestrian is nothing to be ashamed of; in fact, you should feel very proud of yourself for having the gumption to strap yourself to a 1,000-pound prey animal in the first place.

Now, trot on to discover the different things you can do with an English saddle and practice!

Chapter 1: Riding on the Flat

Champion Hunter Under Saddle. Hunt Seat Equitation. Open English Equitation. Handy Hunter. Working Hunter. What do all of these mean?

When researching the various forms of English riding online, you'll likely find terms like these, especially when looking at various show bills, or a training barn may proudly enthuse about their skills in these areas. It sounds great, but what do all of these words translate to in terms of riding?

English classes are broken into two sub-categories: over fences and on the flat. As the name implies, "over fences" means jumping, as in jumping over fences. Flat classes mean the exact opposite— there are no fences, and the class takes place on flat ground.

There are two different areas of focus in English riding. The first is the horse. A hunt seat horse should have an open shoulder, a long, even stride, a steady temperament, and precise transitions between gaits.

The second focus is the rider. The term "equitation" has long been thought to refer only to a rider's position, but the meaning of the word goes a lot deeper. Yes, a magnificently lowered heel, a steady seat, and that ramrod straight spine are important, but true equitation involves riders finding a position that is most effective for a particular horse. Equitation does not mean shoving your body into a position and locking it there. In fact, locking your body so it doesn't move is the last thing your horse wants.

True equitation involves a secure, balanced rider who is able to coax a stunning performance out of their horse without obvious kicking, yanking, and cursing. The horse seems to respond to psychic cues from the rider to change direction, transition from one gait to another, and even perform complicated patterns without either party appearing to put a whole lot of effort into it. As a trainer once explained to me, "Equitation is when you just happen to do everything right, and you look amazing doing it."

So, what's with the many iterations of hunter flat options? Essentially, they all boil down to the same type of riding. Hunt seat horses are expected to have a long, low, and relaxed frame. "Even" and "steady" are the two buzzwords commonly associated with the hunter ring. Some hunters may focus strictly on rail work, meaning they ride around the exterior of an arena at walk, trot, canter, and sometimes hand gallop, usually with at least one change of rein– show speak for "change direction." Other classes require riders to complete a pattern which can include a variety of options such as making a circle, changing leads in the canter, weaving between cones, and even hopping over small jumps.

You don't have to show in order to enjoy hunter-style riding. You can work on creating a smooth, even, steady gait at walk, trot, and canter from the comfort of your own barn. Exercises such as ground poles will help establish balance in both yourself and your horse. You'll want to concentrate on encouraging your horse to move through his entire body, keeping his spine long and loose from his poll (where the spine connects to the skull between his ears) to his tail.

Hunter flat riding is as much about creating an elegant aesthetic as encouraging and sustaining movement that is balanced and regulated. This sort of consistency isn't natural for humans or horses; therefore, while you might think hunt seat is "easier" than disciplines that include a course or a test, your core muscles and glutes might beg to differ after your first lesson. That's what makes flat riding a key component to all of the English disciplines, and a basis for the next several sports we'll discuss.

Chapter 2 : Dressage

Somewhere along the line, dressage gained a reputation for being the snootiest equine discipline. Maybe it's because the sport itself requests absolute perfection from the horse and rider. Maybe it's because of the pristine white breeches, black tail coats, and satin top hats that used to be worn for high level competition. I personally think it's the fact that top level champion dressage horses cost more than my mortgage, but that might be just a touch of jealousy oozing out.

Dressage is definitely my thing. I've always wanted to learn dressage, and once I finally found a program that fit my needs, I immediately stopped doing everything else so I could learn more. Fear not– I'm not going to proselytize on the topic of "horse dancing." Though I personally believe everyone should try it, I appreciate that some people prefer a sport that has black and white versions of success and failure.

Dressage is, for lack of a better word, multi-dimensional. Some may say "impossible," because it truly is impossible to get a perfect score on a dressage test. However, if you step back from the competition aspect, it's really a matter of developing an exquisite relationship with your horse and an appreciation for movement. It really is dancing, with a horse and rider as partners.

A dressage test consists of a variety of movements. These movements can include walk, trot, and canter at various tempos, in which the horse "collects," or contains energy for little forward movement, or "extends," by moving forward expressively. These gaits are performed along the border of the arena, in circles of various sizes, or in serpentine patterns. There are lateral movements in which the horse moves sideways towards and away from the outer borders of the dressage ring, rapid-fire lead changes, and even feats of balance and poise, as in the piaffe, where a horse trots in place for several strides in a row.

Dressage tests are ridden in an arena marked with letters. These letters are placed at regular metered intervals along the outside walls, and along the centerline of the arena as well, though most arenas don't have markers in the middle of the dirt.

It is alleged that these letters originated from the markers that indicated where individuals of importance, such as the king's courier, would expect to receive their horses in Germany's Imperial Court. This certainly seems a reasonable explanation, but generations of riders since have used various mnemonics to remember the seemingly random selection of letters that appear every few meters in a dressage ring. The distance between letters depends on whether the test is ridden in a standard arena or a small arena, which in turn depends on the level of test being ridden.

The levels begin with tests that explore the horse and rider aptitude at skills that are taught early in training such as walking, halting, and trotting. Each subsequent level introduces movements that require greater fitness and ability to execute, with movements occurring faster and with more difficulty in transitioning from one to another.

But here's the catch: you're being judged on how well you do it. According to the [United States Dressage Federation website](), the following qualities are top priority in dressage:

- *Gaits: The freedom and regularity.*
- *Impulsion: Desire to move forward, elasticity of the steps, suppleness of the back, and engagement of the hindquarters.*
- *Submission: The horse's attention and confidence, lightness and ease of movements, acceptance of the bridle, lightness of the forehand, and straightness.*
- *Rider's position and seat.*
- *Rider's correctness and effect of the aid.*

When I say dressage "requests perfection," I mean that each movement is scored from 1-10, with 1 meaning it wasn't good at all to 10 being "excellent." The points are then totaled up and calculated as a percentage of the total possible points. If the movements in a test totalled 100 points, for example, earning 60 out of 100 points would translate into a test score of 60%.

Judges are also encouraged to write notes to explain their scoring, so that riders have an idea of what they can work on in the future. Perfection isn't expected at all; in fact, scores of 60-70% are considered proficient enough for the duo to move up to the next level.

So, why participate in a sport where you can't possibly achieve perfection? For me, the best part of dressage is that I'm only as good as I am at any given moment. It really is a matter of doing the best you can and seeing how your best in this exact test compares to the test you rode yesterday, last week, or last year. Each ride we have is different because each day is different. The horse may be feeling grumpy. The rider might have a stiff neck from sleeping poorly the night before. Still, they perform the movements to the best of their ability in hopes that they will continue to grow in their partnership. In my opinion, it's poetic and affirming.

Plus, there are practical applications to dressage. The sport was created by Greek military riders to display their uniform riding mastery. Other military legions around the world picked up the training as a way to ensure all horses and riders were able to develop to the same standard of athleticism and cunning when going into battle as well. The Imperial Spanish Riding School of Vienna, which was created in 1572, is perhaps one of the most famous examples of classical dressage riding still in existence today. The famous Lipizzaner Stallions train at this facility and demonstrate the discipline as it was intended to be ridden in the Renaissance era. A mounted militia isn't as important to the modern world as it was many centuries ago; therefore, dressage has developed into a test of creating smooth, seamless, cooperative movement. The rider's cues to the horse should be nearly invisible, and the horse should respond in agreement. Precision in execution of each movement leads to higher skills.

This type of training can benefit any horse and rider pair. Dressage encourages horse and rider to use all of their muscles simultaneously to propel them with grace and accuracy. In fact, I liken dressage more to yoga than dancing since the key to success is being able to activate and relax all of your body parts at once. Every shift of balance and pressure from the rider from a squeeze of the thigh to a nudge of the heel, has a different meaning, and yet, the rider must breathe and be at ease. As my trainer has mentioned many times, dressage is the art of turning as little action as possible into the most beautiful movement possible.

The top complaint I hear is that dressage is boring. I can see this point of view because to the untrained eye, nothing is really happening. But the act of riding dressage, when one puts in the effort to assist their horse in moving comfortably and correctly, while maintaining a peaceful and cooperative connection, is an act that requires almost zen-like patience and a full admission of your own fallibility.

At the higher levels of dressage, riders use a specialized dressage saddle. These are typically black, deep seated saddles with long flaps that extend under the rider's thigh and calf. The goal is to allow the rider to position themselves in a way that permits them to follow the movement of the muscles in the horse's back, increasing the sensitivity of the seat. This means that even small amounts of pressure from the rider become "invisible" cues, leading to the illusion that horse and rider are working together via psychic connection.

However, you don't need any specific equipment (or any equipment at all) to work on harmony and forward motion at all gaits. I encourage every equestrian to try the basics of dressage, as it has the potential to break down a lot of resistance that you and your horse may be encountering while learning another discipline. Consider it couples counseling for you and your horse!

Chapter 3 : Jumping

You'd be hard pressed to find someone who isn't impressed with the aerial feats of riders and horses soaring over obstacles. For a brief moment, it's as if Pegasus manifested, and flying on the back of a noble steed is a real possibility. Defying gravity, they propel above the ground, then gracefully touch down on the other side.

Or not. Navigating a large, opinionated beast around a set course of obstacles which must be taken in a specific order, often within a specific time limit, is an activity with little room for error. If a horse doesn't feel comfortable jumping, they'll stop before they have to. Most of the time, the rider's momentum will carry them over the fence without the horse, resulting in at least a dirty face and bruised ego. Horses can also misjudge the height or distance they need to jump and clip a rail or stumble upon landing. There's also the chance of the dreaded rotational fall, in which the horse essentially somersaults head-first over a fence. Jumping is dangerous, but many riders agree that the feeling of flying far outweighs the fear of falling.

A common misconception is that jumping is easy. The horse does all the work, right? While it's true that the horse is in charge of carrying himself and the rider over the fence, the rider is responsible for helping the horse get to and over the fence as safely and correctly as possible. In jumping, the term "correct" refers to maintaining enough momentum in between fences to propel the duo over each obstacle and finding a good "distance" or spot from which the horse can take off.

The goal is to set your horse up so that the span and apex of the jump give him enough room to clear the obstacle so that he doesn't hit a rail or bring down a fence with an errant hoof. One of my trainers explained it, "The horsey flies, but the horsey won't fly well if you don't ride well."

Jumping is difficult, but also incredibly rewarding. The first time you pop over a cross-rail, you get that miniscule moment of being weightless combined with the knowledge that you just made a horse fly. The adrenaline rush is exquisite, and the amount of mental and physical prowess required to get through a course well is a challenge many riders thoroughly enjoy.

There are several different types of jumping as well, each of which brings a different perspective to the concept of getting a horse over an obstacle.

Hunter Jumpers

As an extension of hunt seat riding on the flat, hunter jumpers are expected to go around a course of fences with the same steady, even stride.

Generally speaking, the jump courses for hunter rounds aren't super complex. The jumps are set at heights that typically range from eighteen inches to three feet, six inches. Jumps increase in height in increments of three inches, so a 2'0" rider will progress to a 2'3" course, and so on. The most common fence type is a regular vertical, or a fence that consists of two standards and a pole. Oxers, or obstacles that are both wide and high, are not uncommon in higher levels of competition and can include verticals set closely together to form a single jump effort or solid-appearing objects such as rolltops, coops, and flower boxes. I've included more information on hunter courses in the "Resources" section, if you'd like to explore more.

The most common course design, especially for lower levels, includes two outside lines and two fences on the inside diagonal line, meaning the pattern resembles a figure-8. There are a few deviations from this standard, of course, but the point of the course is to demonstrate the horse's ability to present a forward, even, and balanced stride on both canter leads, including at least one lead change. "Lead" is the term used for the leg that leads when the horse is cantering- the inside leg should be the one that strikes the ground first when the horse is cantering. A lead change, therefore, means changing direction, and thus, changing which leg is leading.

Over the fences, the horses should present themselves as sharp, strong, and capable. This ideal includes high, tightly tucked knees, and a rounded spine that indicates the horse is using his entire body to clear the obstacle. The rider's goal is to ensure an even and exact number of strides between the fences, with the horse presenting a uniform athletic effort over each fence.

Equitation is highly emphasized in hunter jumpers. The rider is expected to maintain a soft, following hand, with open shoulder angles, and an open hip that allows the horse to use his entire body to power over the fence. Heels should be down and aligned with the hip to provide balance and stability through the arch of the jump. To all appearances, the rider should simply be floating along on the horse's back, going with the motion instead of interfering.

The overall concept to keep in mind for hunters is "minimalism." The riders dress in plain black or navy jackets with beige or white breeches, tall black dress boots, and hair neatly hidden in a hunt cap. Saddles and bridles are plain, and if a saddle pad is used, it is generally plain white. The idea is to remove all distinctive features so the judge can focus on the movement and performance of the horse and rider. I'd like to add that, despite what you may see on television and in movies, hunter jumpers don't wear the hunt coat every single time they ride- only in the show ring.

Those coats are expensive, hard to clean, and often super hot and stuffy, like a suit jacket. Most riders don't enjoy wearing them unless it's absolutely necessary.

Regardless of whether you wear a coat or even consider entering a show ring, training for hunter jumper courses can be a great way to build fitness in you and your horse. One way in which hunters achieve this fitness is by schooling– what we call our at-home practice rides– over gymnastics or jump sets in which each obstacle immediately precedes the next. This builds core muscle for horse and human and develops the roundness and athleticism required to snap those knees high and arch roundly over each fence. I've put some examples in the "Resources" section so you can see for yourself if this is something you and your pony would like to try.

Show Jumping

Many people are introduced to show jumping via the Summer Olympics as it is one of the few equestrian sports that is regularly televised. In 2021, Olympic Show Jumping received an extra dose of attention, as rock legend Bruce Springsteen's daughter, Jessica Springsteen, rode on the silver medal-winning United States team. People who had never really considered the world of equestrian sports were suddenly made aware of a sport in which people willingly rode their horses at top speed towards and over weird-looking obstacles measuring over five feet in height and up to six feet, five inches in width. On top of that, the horse and rider team who completes the course fastest with the fewest poles down wins. Even non-horsey people can be sucked into rooting for a particular duo as they watch horse and rider teams charge boldly at behemoth jumps.

Not all show jumping courses include fences over five feet, or 1.6 meters now that the Fédération Equestre Internationale (FEI) is officially using the metric system in course guides. Like any other sport, beginners start out over smaller fences, and as they gain comfort and ability at the sport, the fences become larger.

Some people think of show jumping as the "opposite" of hunters since hunter-jumpers focus on form and presence, while show jumpers aim for a clear round in which no fences or poles are pulled down when the horse goes over the jumps, in the fastest time. It doesn't really matter *how* a show jumper gets around the course or what their equitation looks like, just that they land the last fence alive and well.

Of course, that's a bit of a hyperbolic look at show jumpers, as they are fantastically athletic, with swiftness to carry them rapidly along the flat ground winding between the jumps. They have the agility to adjust their stride to spring high into the air and land gracefully over a dozen fences.

While hunter classes are designed to display a horse's athleticism through perfect repetition, a show jumping course requires the horse and rider to solve problems. This can include weird distances between fences, which can require adjusting your speed and tempo with each stride, tight turns, bending lines, and combination fences, in which the horse jumps a fence, has two or three strides to gather himself before the next fence of equal height, then one stride upon landing in order to prepare for the third fence in the group. Don't forget you're trying to jump them without knocking anything over. And do it faster than the last guy!

Show jumping looks hard because it is hard, and I'm pretty excited that it's finally getting national recognition. On the other hand, I imagine some people find it discouraging that you can't just start show jumping. First, you need to learn how to ride, then get the basics of jumping under your belt, have the physical fitness required to contain 1,000 pounds of raw energy, holding it back and pushing it as needed in order to quickly get through a twisted, winding maze of fences. I'm afraid you aren't going to be show jumping in your first lesson. You can become a show jumper— just not overnight. Give it at least a few years.

However, the concepts involved in show jumping are fantastic for building athleticism and agility in any horse. One of my favorite exercises for any horse is to build a show jumping course out of poles laid on the ground. It doesn't actually have to make sense— the beauty of this exercise is that you are going to be adjusting your horse to remain balanced and forward even when taking impossibly tight turns and uneven distances. Doing this exercise at a walk is a great way to help horses loosen up and move forward at the walk, which is when most horses enjoy seeing how lazy we'll let them be. Red is famous for shuffling along at the walk until he trips, so I'll do this exercise at the trot first, then make him walk over poles until it occurs to him that he can pick up his feet just a little more.

If words like big, fast, and "whee!" are attractive to you, then you might be interested in learning more about show jumping opportunities in your area. I've included some links in the "Resources" section to help you get started.

Cross Country / Three Day Eventing

The terms "cross country" and "eventing" are often used interchangeably, though they don't quite mean the same thing. Cross country is one of the stages of three day eventing, which to complicate matters more is also known as "combined training," or "horse trials" as it combines three different activities into one competition.

Three day eventing is an equestrian sport that, as the name implies, takes part in three phases. At introductory levels, the three phases are completed in the same day, but at FEI and Olympic levels, the events take place on three separate days to allow horses and riders to recuperate between challenges.

Why three different sports in one? The goal of three day eventing is to demonstrate the athletic prowess of horse and rider. Essentially, this is the equine triathlon. Established as a sport back when the cavalry held demonstrations of their skills and capabilities, eventing has gone through many changes over the years; however, it remains a test of will, determination, talent, bravery, and yes, the ability to run fast and jump scary things.

The first event is dressage. The concept of dressage within the context of eventing is the same as that within dressage as a stand alone discipline: the horse and rider must convey the impression that they are silently, magically, and mysteriously dancing as one. Horse and rider pairs are scored on quality of gait, balance and suppleness in turns and transitions, collection and extension, engagement, and harmony between horse and rider.

The movements that are requested in the test are less based on classical dressage, but rooted in demonstrating the ability for horse and rider to communicate practically. Piaffe and passage are not part of eventing dressage; instead, you'll find plenty of transitions, circles, half-passes, collection and extension, and riding to and out of the halt.

Next is cross country… usually. There are different formats to different three day events depending on the size, the levels of competition included in the event, and the organization holding the show. Some smaller shows present stadium jumping as the second event. Larger events have road and tracks and steeplechase segments in which horses are asked to gallop across the countryside and sail over fences within a certain amount of time. The most popular version is the "short" event in which the second event asks horse and rider to gallop across open land, tree-lined trails, over bridges, through water, and more in the exciting cross country jumping round.

I encourage you to check out some of the videos included in the "Resources" section to gain a sense of how much bravery and athleticism is required of horse and rider in the upper levels of eventing. It's not the size of the fence that's as intimidating as the fact that each obstacle asks a lot of questions of the horse and rider. You may approach a jump in the middle of running up or down a hill, meaning your take off and landing are two different heights. You may jump off a bank into a pool of water, then jump another bank upwards out of the water. The obstacles are usually based on things you would find when galloping around your own backyard- logs, ditches, creeks, abandoned objects, walls, fences, or small houses. And each obstacle is just as solid as it looks with no room for error. It's easy to be intimidated by the potential for failure.

The last phase of three day eventing is stadium jumping. This is very similar to show jumping in that horse and rider are back in the ring, competing over a course of fences to see who has the clearest round in the fastest time. At this point, horse and rider are tired, running on the last vestiges of adrenaline, and potentially wondering if they could back track their decision making process to the moment when this sounded like a good idea. Still, they persevere by navigating a technically difficult course of jumps.

At the end of the three events, each pair's score is tallied, and the horse and rider with the fewest errors are declared the winners. That is a very simplistic explanation of how eventing scoring works, but explaining all of the various coefficients and penalty awards for each different format of eventing by each ruling committee is practically its own college major, let alone a book!

Is eventing for you? You will know. Just as it takes a very specific set of abilities to compete in a human triathlon, three day eventing requires training, discipline, and commitment, not to mention heaps and heaps of bravery. It is truly a sport in which each step must be calculated and purposeful, and both horse and rider must be able to deal with a variety of rapidly-changing scenarios. Accuracy is the key to success, along with the ability to adapt quite literally mid-stride to accommodate error or misjudgement. It requires an amount of skill and patience that I greatly admire.

There is great benefit in schooling outdoors, and over even small fences in strange places. Many riders have encountered a fallen tree while on a trail ride and had to make a quick decision about how to proceed. Furthermore, training for endurance and adaptability can benefit every horse and rider. That being said, I recommend you do any attempted eventing under the tutelage of a trained professional, because when things go wrong in eventing, they can be fatal.

But if that doesn't scare you off, there's very likely a cross country course near you just waiting for you to try it!

Field Hunting

You know those old paintings you see, of red-coated riders and stoic brown horses jumping over fences, hedges, and tearing through the woods after a pack of hound dogs? That's known as field hunting which is linked to more low-key versions of the sport such as hunter paces.

In the original sport, a group of riders mounted up to ceremoniously chase a fox across the countryside. The expectation was that the excursion would last all day. In fact, several riders are employed to help guide the hunting dogs through terrain that makes the sport even more fun and daring for the riders. At its root, this type of hunting was more of a social event between neighboring equestrians than a survivalist search for food, with traditions such as a pre-hunt breakfast and a post-hunt feast, along with several pit stops along the way for conviviality.

Historically speaking, only male riders were permitted to ride astride, with one leg on each side of the horse. Women rode "aside", or sidesaddle. In fact, riding astride as a female only became normalized in Western culture as recently as the 1930s! Today, there are quite a few riders who continue the tradition of riding sidesaddle, and in modern day riding, men are invited to ride aside as well.

Social implications of the sport aside, field hunting and its offshoot trials and paces are known for their good-natured social aspect, rather than serving as a staunch competition. Though some of these sports offer prizes and placement, most riders participate for the thrill of riding across the countryside and finding new and exciting obstacles to navigate over, around, and through.

Though the paintings from the 1800s depict a pack of riders heading at full-tilt, most field hunting involves a significant amount of walking and trotting, as the terrain and weather permit. Mud is a familiar factor, and hunters in the United States typically gather in the fall and winter months when there are fewer leaves on the trees. There may be a lot of standing around and waiting, especially if there are hounds involved. Some field gatherings offer different groups centered around skill level and comfort riding in the open, which allows each group to set a pace that works for everyone.

Still, the full-tilt thing does happen, and that's what makes the whole thing thrilling. The trees turn to a brownish-gray blur as you pick up speed, as you brace yourself against wind, rain, and the possibility of getting smacked in the face by twigs and low-hanging branches. The pursuit can last for a good stretch of time before the pack slows once again, but it won't be long until the hunt is back on.

"Hunting" at home is one of the most common activities among young equestrians, especially those with bold ponies and a large pasture, field, or trail system to explore on their own property. I have particularly fond memories of watching a bunch of kids in rubber boots hop on their ponies bareback to hunt through the woods for one of the barn cats, whose name just happened to be Foxy.

This is not to sound dismissive of hunting at all– in order to successfully participate, you need the bravery of a three day eventer, the endurance to stay on horseback for an entire day, the sense of adventure to purposefully get lost, and the skillful equitation that can help you ride through any potential mess. Then, add in the general excitement of the pack and the braying of the hounds, and you have an experience that will challenge every aspect of your equestrian knowledge.

What separates field hunting from trail riding or plain old-fashioned goofing off on a horse? There's a great deal of ceremony and tradition involved in hunting, and there are rules that give it an air of organization. But I suspect underneath all of the pomp and circumstance, we're all inclined to ride off into the sunset, regardless of whether we're in pursuit of a fox, a barn cat, or our own imagination. So, whether you join a local pack or invent one in your backyard, why not sneak in a little hunt now and again to test your bravery and horsemanship?

Hunt Seat in a Nutshell

Yes, that's a lot of information to take in at once. Just as Rome wasn't built in a day, no one has learned all of these disciplines and activities at once. Even three day eventers take three days to complete their phases.

Again, this information isn't intended to be taken as professional instruction but more as an inspiration as you and your horse work to find your stride together. Whether you're looking for new ways to play together at home or searching for a career that will put you on the track for professional status, these are a sample of some of the popular hunt seat sports practiced around the world.

Now let's take a walk on the Western side, and check out what the cowboys are doing.

SECTION 2 : THE WESTERN DISCIPLINES

Some Western riders aim to separate themselves from the cowboy heritage from which the riding style evolved. Others make it a robust lifestyle.

There certainly is something appealing about the imagery of the Wild West. There's a certain amount of do-it-yourself attitude, mixed with utter lawlessness, and the freedom that comes with being 200 miles away from anything. Especially with so many of today's population working in tightly-packed offices and living in close reach of our neighbors in condos and apartment complexes, the vision of watching the sunset from the back of a horse while the cows graze peacefully in the distance is pretty ideal.

You don't need a herd of cattle to enjoy all of the disciplines that fall under the Western umbrella, though. Many of these sports were developed around all of the other practical riding that happens when you're taking care of a farm. You've got the low, flat, and comfortable gaits that were developed for all-day riding. There are activities that test your ability to navigate through expected obstacles as well as those that require you to ride hell-bent for leather like someone's after your hide. As we dig deeper into the Western disciplines, it will become clear that these are sports built out of purpose, though over time, they've become more stylized than what you might expect at the typical working ranch.

One thing that unifies each of the following activities is the saddle. While the English saddle is flat and allows for plenty of hip movement when hunting and racing, the Western saddle is deep with a longer, straighter leg position. This allows for stability and comfort, whether you're riding for a long time or dealing with fast, rapidly changing movements as you might expect when chasing a stray dogie. From this position, an open hip, well-developed core, and soft seat will allow Western riders to remain in place, allowing the horse to do his work.

Western saddles have a distinctive "horn" on the front. This horn comes in various shapes and sizes, depending on its function. It can be used to stabilize a rider while the horse makes lightning-fast adjustments, or you can hang various equipment, such as ropes and saddle bags from it. While Western saddles may look uniform, they can be specifically designed to improve a rider's ability to perform certain jobs– such as the high pommel on a roping saddle. However, a general work saddle will be sufficient for entry-level riding and trying out a few different activities.

Western riding also requires far less contact between the rider's hands and the bit in the horse's mouth than English riding does. In Western riding, the bits are often larger and heavier. The horse is trained to appreciate smaller and softer shifts of the bit. This means the rider can ride on a looser rein. In practical application, this means a rider's hands are more free to open gates, rope cattle, or eat a sandwich, depending on what the day's work brings.

The following chapters will give you an overview of the slow and low, the fast and furious, and all the pattern classes in between that comprise the Western riding disciplines. Take a look and decide for yourself what you and your horse might like to try.

Chapter 1: Pleasure and Patterns

There's something about the balance and effortlessness of the Western jog that I absolutely adore. Legs long and hips open, your seat rocks in an almost imperceivable side to side motion.

Of course, there's way more to it than that. Highly competitive riders know how to accomplish the headset, and the right amount of pause between strides that gives a pleasure horse the most pleasant-appearing gaits. The tiny shifts of balance that happen in the hands to encourage the horse to steer are admirable.

If hunt seat disciplines are divided into "on the flat " and "jumping," then Western disciplines can be divided into Pleasure, Pattern, and Performance. Like hunter classes, Pleasure tends to focus on the horse's performance and appearance. Pattern classes require serious communication between horse and rider, while Performance classes focus on how quickly a horse and rider duo can complete various patterns or tasks. Let's take a look at each.

Western Pleasure

Western pleasure correlates to the hunter on the flat activities that we discussed earlier; the primary difference is the saddle, but there's far more to it than that. While hunt seat riders are encouraged to move forward with open, even, steady gaits, Western riders prefer a slower, more controlled, flat-kneed gait. That's not to say that Western horses *can't* go fast– they are horses, after all– but that they are trained and often bred to produce a range of gaits that are all-day comfortable for both horse and rider.

There are several different activities that traditionally fall under the Western pleasure umbrella. The first is rail work. Rail work is basically what most people do in their lessons or warm up. You walk around the outside of the arena, then jog, lope, switch direction, and do it all again. Sometimes things get exciting, such as multiple changes of direction or walk-to-lope transitions.

Generally speaking, judges in Western pleasure competitions are not looking so much at the rider as the horse. They want to see quality gaits, and an obedient, quiet horse. In breed shows, such as those of the Appaloosa Horse Club, the American Paint Horse Registry, or the American Quarter Horse Association, just to name a few, judges will also focus on how well the horse represents the breed standard.

One question I've heard frequently is, "What is up with the Western pleasure outfits?" Mostly, these words are spoken in awe and fascination. While hunt seat riders are relegated to the muted palette of black, gray, navy, white, and beige, Western pleasure riders are decked out in colorful, bejeweled jackets and brightly colored chaps with long, decadent fringe. Their saddles are slathered with shiny bits of silver, and their coordinated saddle pads are brightly patterned.

This is part of the pageantry that is common in Western shows within the United States. Not all Western disciplines subscribe to this dress code, however. Working classes, such as ranch riding, speed events, reining, and roping, all have a more function-based dress code. Generally, riders in those classes will wear a button down shirt, jeans, chaps, and cowboy boots.

So what's up with the "blinged-out" riders? There are various theories as to where the style originated. Some say it started when horse people from remote farms would meet up in their Sunday best to show off their horses to each other. Others say it's a natural evolution of the suit-style clothing that pleasure riders wore to demonstrate that their horse's gaits were so smooth, they didn't kick up dust.

Most modern riders work for months to create a full custom turnout that will compliment and enhance their horse's appearance. Everything coordinates in a color that contrasts perfectly with the horse's coat. While the horse's coat is polished to an almost mirror-like sheen, the rhinestones in the rider's jacket illuminate their presence with the reflective twinkle of tiny lights.

Watching a high-stakes class like the AQHA Masters can be a festival of lights and colors, making it a truly breathtaking thing to behold. Bear in mind that the pageant is exclusive to the show ring. Much as hunt seat riders rarely wear hunt coats outside of the ring, Pleasure riders school in regular old clothes. In fact, the silver-studded saddles often sit in a place of pride until show weekend arrives. You don't need special equipment to get started with Western pleasure schooling– just a horse.

Horsemanship

Western Horsemanship is, on paper, the opposite of rail work. This class judges a rider's equitation, along with the harmony between horse and rider. Horsemanship is somewhat like dressage, in that horse and rider pairs are asked to perform a series of movements and tasks in order, which challenge their ability to communicate clearly with each other. However, while dressage tests take place in a lettered arena, Horsemanship classes often have cones or other markers to designate where certain movements in the pattern should start and stop. Riders may be asked to ride circles, transition between various gaits, change leads or direction, and back up throughout a horsemanship pattern.

The precision in movements required to complete a Horsemanship pattern accurately is something anyone who works with horses should attempt. Reading the instructions, it doesn't seem too difficult. Take the first three directions of the 2012 AQHA Select World (Finals) Horsemanship as an example:

1. Walk 15 feet
2. Extended jog to middle of arena
3. 360-degree turn to the left followed by 360-degree turn to the right

However, being able to set up for a 360-degree turn right out of a fairly fast jog means knowing exactly where you and your horse's bodies need to be in order to make a seamless, accurate transition. Oh yeah, and the rider's equitation is being judged every step of the way. No pressure!

Horsemanship requires riders to communicate quickly and effectively with their horses. As you'll see from the example tests included in the "Resources" section, each pattern has a different level of difficulty. At the competitive level, you'll likely get a copy of your pattern just a few hours before you enter the ring which adds an extra level of anxiety to the class.

As a result, many Horsemanship riders school as many different patterns as they can find online. The result is clean, careful, and consistent communication between horse and rider, which we should all strive towards, regardless of discipline.

Should you work on these patterns at home, I recommend working on getting the feel for the movements and work involved in executing each movement, then putting them together as a full pattern. Then, only once you and your horse have the idea down, focus on your body position. And don't let frustration win— this is an experience, not an automatic process.

The pattern-based activities continue with Trail, Ranch Riding, and Western Dressage. These terms are sometimes confused with each other or used interchangeably, so it's not uncommon for newer riders to become confused by these three. Let's take a look at each.

Trail

Not to be confused with riding on a trail, Trail classes usually take place in an arena. When riders approach the arena, they will notice a lot of stuff seemingly scattered randomly around almost every inch of the usable ground. Welcome to Trail!

Like Horsemanship, Trail classes challenge horse and rider by requiring them to ride a course. This isn't a jump course, however, though there may be some small cross rails or natural-styled obstacles like logs to hop over. Mostly, these classes test the ability of the horse and rider to communicate successfully while maneuvering over lines of poles, through gates, around poles, and over small platforms known as "bridges." Horse and rider pairs may be asked to walk, trot, lope, or even navigate these obstacles in reverse.

One famous Trail obstacle that I have been asked to practice seemingly millions of times as a young rider, and which I still use today is the "Dog Leg." This obstacle is created by four poles, set parallel to each other, with a 120-degree angle between the two of them. When set up correctly, it will resemble a very open letter "L" or a dog's hind leg. Riders are asked to walk, trot, or lope through the poles, then stop and navigate through the bend in reverse. The goal is to be able to do this with no hesitation of horse or rider, and without stepping on or over the poles.

You don't actually need poles to do this— you can draw lines in the dirt for a very cost-effective version- but you do need a lot of patience. In fact, you might wonder the first few times if it can be done. The secret to success is simply relaxing, thinking ahead, planning carefully, and not over-steering your horse.

This aim for accuracy is the entire point of Trail riding. The idea is to mimic things horse and rider might encounter out on an actual trail, such as opening a gate between fence lines, winding around tightly-planted trees, and stepping over fallen branches or logs in rapid fire succession without losing your footing or concentration.

Many riding instructors feel that schooling these types of obstacles are fantastic for building communication skills and learning how to take one challenge at a time, and I agree. The idea of going over a pole at any gait might seem ridiculously simple, until your horse doesn't pick up his feet and trips over it. While it's unlikely that you or your horse will fall, it will still provide a jarring reminder of how much you rely on each other's balance and coordination. At a trot or lope, going over a line of poles— meaning, several poles in a row with the same number of strides in between them— will require the horse to engage different parts of his body to keep moving in a balanced manner without losing their stride and rhythm. If one of you loses their concentration, it will soon be evident in the clatter of poles.

While you may never desire the Trail class blue ribbon, I highly encourage you to explore some of the Trail obstacles, many of which can be easily created at home. In fact, this is one case where the more rugged materials you use, the more realistic your experience will be!

Ranch Work

Ranch Work essentially takes the concept of Horsemanship, throws a few obstacles into the mix like Trail, and then adds cows. At least, that is how most classes at upper level shows unfold.

Ranch classes are sometimes known as Versatility classes depending on what is being asked of the horse and rider. At some shows, Ranch classes are more of an extreme version of Horsemanship and Trail put together, meaning riders are expected to ride both an equitation-based pattern while going through a course of obstacles. Riders may also be asked to perform "working" gaits, such as the extended jog and extended lope, which ask the horse to take bigger strides with greater impulsion from their hindquarters. It's definitely a sport that requires a lot physically and mentally from horse and rider.

Much as the name implies, Ranch riding mimics what a horse and rider would encounter if they were a working team on a cattle ranch. As a result, some classes involve navigating through and around a pen of cows, though you may or may not have to interact with them. The goal is to demonstrate that the horse has no problem being in the midst of many bovine, and that he remains tuned in to what the rider is asking of him.

So, while all of this is going on in the ring, what are judges looking for? In a nutshell, they're looking for a pair that looks like they'd be right at home on a ranch. Horses are expected to approach each obstacle in stride. They should look comfortable and at ease with no tail swishing or ear pinning. The gaits should be even and the transitions smooth. If a horse stops or refuses to work with an obstacle, it's a penalty.

The great news about Ranch riding is that you can practice at home with very little extra equipment. Some poles will be helpful, and you likely have a gate somewhere that you can practice riding up to, unlatching, walking through, and latching behind you. Many Ranch riding patterns are also available online, which means you can practice the precise transitions, extensions, and turns that are required in competition. You definitely don't ever have to leave home to practice some of the finer points of this riding style.

Western Dressage

Western Dressage has been around as long as people have been sitting in Western saddles, but it has only recently gained recognition as a competitive discipline. I remember watching my first Western Dressage clinic and wondering aloud to a friend whether it was "dressage with a horn." To a certain extent, it truly is.

Many credit trainers Tom and Bill Dorrance with the development of modern Western Dressage. Combining the grace of Classical Dressage and the flexibility and balance required within Horsemanship patterns, the goal of the sport is to encourage lightness, forward motion, and balance. The Dorrance brothers initially formulated dressage-based training techniques as a way to create a mental and physical bond between horses of any breed and riders of all backgrounds that could result in a long, healthy relationship and working career.

And then it took off! Western Dressage is now recognized by the American Quarter Horse Association (AQHA) and the United States Equestrian Federation (USEF). Trainers across the country are specializing in Western Dressage, making the sport increasingly available for riders everywhere.

Much as in classical dressage, Western Dressage horse and rider teams are asked to ride a test composed of several different movements that demonstrate forward, fluid working gaits. Conceptually, based on movements that a working Ranch horse might need to execute when working, the tests range from Intro to Level 5. Horse and rider duos may be asked to walk, jog, lope, and demonstrate collection and extension in those gaits. Pivots, pirouettes, half-passes, circles, and serpentines are added to illustrate the team's suppleness and harmony.

Western Dressage is something every horse and rider can benefit from, as its principles require keen communication between you and your beast. Practicing skills that require balance, flexibility, and forwardness can help you find solutions for big challenges, regardless of what disciplines you normally ride. And while Western Dressage tests generally take place in a lettered arena, just like hunt seat dressage, you really don't need anything to start trying out some of the test movements on your own. Practice forward, collaborative gaits, straight lines, and circles, or download one of the online tests provided by the Western Dressage Association of America (WDAA). Don't focus on making the ride look perfect– focus on having the best possible ride for you and your horse.

Pleasure and Pattern riding is the bread and butter of the Western disciplines. The Performance sports– which we'll look at next– require riders to be steady and capable in both Pleasure and Pattern riding in order to pull off the athletic demands of each sport. While these disciplines may not seem as high-adrenaline as speed events, they are challenging, as horse and rider are constantly asked to challenge their skills and ability each stride of the way.

Chapter 2 : High Performance Western Sports

The title of this chapter is not to imply that there isn't a high level of performance and passion involved with other Western disciplines but that these particular sports add the elements of speed and agility to the skills built upon in Pleasure and Pattern type classes.

Though we're barely scraping the surface of what's involved in each discipline, I hope the following descriptions help get you as amped up about reining and speed events as the competitors themselves. These classes are always a big draw at large shows thanks to the fast-paced, adrenaline-soaked thrills of each competitor's round. Will this horse be faster? Slide further? Or will this horse hit a barrel on their way through the turns? The sense of danger is great, as a single misstep at these high speeds could lead to a major spill.

One of the most admirable qualities of high performance Western sports is the finely tuned communication between horse and rider. Reining horses are trained to perform a pattern in a manner that appears effortless. Contesting horses may seem like fire-breathing locomotives out of the ring, but once the gate opens, they're all business, finding the swiftest place to put each hoof in rapid succession. The rider, meanwhile, urges on their horse in levels of excitement ranging from subtle and synchronistic to so enthusiastic that the pair seems to leave common physics behind as they hover above the ground in pursuit of the fastest time.

Much as show jumping and cross country are considered some of the more high-performance sports performed in an English saddle, reining and contesting would hold similar positions in Western riding, though the purpose and nuances of each sport are different.   Read on to determine if you and your horse are able– or even willing– to pursue these performanced-based Western sports.

Reining

Technically speaking, reining is a pattern-based discipline. However, since the whole pattern is performed at a lope or gallop, this is definitely a high performance element. And when you factor in an arena full of eager spectators whooping and whistling as the horse and rider perform moves like rollbacks, sliding stops, and spins, the adrenaline really starts pumping.

At the basis of every reining pattern is the demonstration of being able to ride a smooth, forward circle of various sizes and at different speeds, as well as being able to gallop in straight lines, ending with the physics-defying, seemingly zero-friction, sliding stop. Add into the mix the horse making rapid spins while planted on a single hind hoof, all seemingly without a single cue or request from the rider. According to the National Reining Horse Association (NRHA):

"To rein a horse is not only to guide him, but also to control his every movement. The best reined horse should be willingly guided or controlled with little or no apparent resistance and dictated to completely… credit should be given for smoothness, finesse, attitude, quickness and authority of performing various maneuvers, while using controlled speed."

- *2017 NHRA Pattern Guide (https://nrha.com/media/pdf/2017/patterns.pdf) Page 4*

Of course, appearances can be deceiving. Riding a correct reining pattern requires intense concentration on behalf of both horse and rider. Having had the pleasure to work with top-notch professional reiners, I admire their enthusiasm and determination for performing well. The riders are extremely dedicated to their sport, too!

Practicing intermittent slow and fast, large and small circles at every gait is a great exercise for every horse and rider team;. However, I will caution against attempting fast spins or sliding stops without a special hind shoe called a "sliding shoe" or "slider". This type of shoe has a shiny, flat metal surface that allows the horse to glide on arena footing, while their natural hooves provide a certain amount of built-in grip. A horse without sliders can still perform these moves, but he won't be able to replicate the twenty-foot slides you see at the professional level, and it will create a certain amount of wear and tear to his hindlimb joints.

To add a little bit of reining to your training, try seeing how much you can accomplish with the smallest possible cues. This will take lots of practice, but you'll start to discover how clenching the reins, twisting your wrist, or shifting your weight forward or back in the saddle can impact how your horse moves. These principles are what make a reiner look so graceful and at ease and translate well into success in other disciplines as well.

Speed Events

I'd like to start this overview of timed equine events with a confession: I'm not aware of every single mounted speed event. I know of the major ones such as Barrel Racing, Pole Bending, and Mounted Shooting. But then we get into the somewhat uncivilized world of the local Gymkhana and its mix of familiar mounted games and regional competitions that likely evolved from a dare. Nearly every long-time horse person has looked at a show bill in another county or state, pointed at a speed event class name, and asked, "What's that class about?"

While some speed events are sanctioned with distinct rules and regulations, others declare their winner by who arrives at the finish line in one piece the fastest. For some riders, this can sound like terrifying territory. For others, it's the best thing in the whole wide world.

I don't like to generalize, but there are certain people who are confirmed thrill seekers. Some people enjoy skydiving and bungee jumping. Some seek out the tallest, fastest, and scariest roller coasters. Others compete in speed-based riding events. There may be overlap between these groups, as well.

If pattern work is all about precision, speed events only amplify that particular talent. Depending on the size of the arena, a barrel course can be over in anywhere between fifteen and thirty seconds. Allow me to emphasize the word *seconds*. By the time you have finished reading this sentence word for word, a barrel racer will have galloped into the arena, raced at top speed around three barrels in a cloverleaf pattern– which includes at least one lead change– and dashed out of the arena while the crowd loudly cheers them on.

Some speed events are clearly designed as races. Down and Back is an activity that only involves one turn, though the horse and rider are instead responsible for sprinting from the in-gate to the end of the arena, swiftly spin around a single barrel, and practically teleport themselves back to the in-gate at top speed.

Other timed events involve more complicated tasks. Mounted Shooting, for example, requires horse and rider to dash through an arena, riding a pattern while aiming two .45 caliber single action revolvers at up to ten balloons tied to poles. The goal is to shoot as many balloons as possible without having to circle back.

Another fun feature of Mounted Shooting is that the official sport organization, the Cowboy Mounted Shooting Association (CMSA) encourages members to turn back time and dress in attire that wouldn't be out of place in a cowboy movie. Much as field hunting captures the pageantry of Olde England, Mounted Shooting invokes the spirit of the Wild West with collarless shirts, button jeans, and weathered cowboy hats.

If the idea of trying a variety of mounted speed events and conquering many different obstacles while the clock ticks away amuses you, you might seek out a Gymkhana. The definition of Gymkhana is generally accepted to be, "…a variety of mounted speed events and timed obstacles courses," because the classes you might encounter at one can be so varied. In the equestrian world, we joke that Gymkhana is pure lawless thrills, but there are certainly rules to each competition in addition to having the fastest possible time.

You might encounter some of the speed classes previously mentioned at a Gymkhana event, along with some other fascinating races. For example, you and a partner might be asked to race through cones while each holding the opposite end of a swatch of toilet paper. Riders may be asked to balance an egg on a spoon while weaving through poles or completing a pattern based on Horsemanship skills. Back when phone books were large, impressive tomes, riders would race each other to a phone book placed in the far end of an arena with the goal of being the first to tear out a specific page and hustle back to the starting line. These might seem like silly races to have, but they are a true test of one's ability to ride accurately and athletically.

It is almost unheard of in the equestrian community for a rider to not be challenged to a race of some sort by another rider, especially if you happen to keep your horse at a boarding barn with similarly aged and skilled equestrians. I have many happy memories of "pole bending" with my first horse as we wove through a line of jump standards we dragged out from the side of the arena. My large Thoroughbred was only able to trot the maneuvers, because of how tall, long, and gangly he was, while a girl with a small sway-backed pony of undetermined breeding left us in the dust. When it comes to being quick, knowing your center of gravity and the boundaries of what you and your horse can do are often just as important— if not more— than being big and trained to go fast.

One word of caution, however— speed events really can be dangerous, as horses can lose their balance and crash to the ground. I strongly encourage anyone who wants to try these events to get comfortable at all gaits first, then start with trying the patterns at a low speed before going full-out at a dead gallop. You'll note that the organizations associated with these sports have different requirements for riders ranging from beginner to highly experienced, so while it's good to challenge yourself, don't overface yourself. And don't be afraid to wear a helmet!

With Bovine Assistance

The term "cowboy" implies that there are cows somehow involved in Western riding, but so far, we have seen very few actual horned, hooved, milk-producing ruminants. With the exception of the potential for a pen of cattle in Ranch Work, all of these events involve a horse and rider pair.

There's Cutting, Roping, Team Roping, Team Penning, Cattle Working, Ranch Sorting, Reined Cow Horse, and more... It may be difficult for a brand new cowboy to decide where they should put their focus. Each class is a bit different, but success at home, on the range, and in the ring hinges on one very important factor:

Your horse has to be okay with cows.

Technically speaking, any breed can participate in cattle events, from the flashy Andalusian horses that appear at the end of a bullfight to the rough-and-ready American stock horse. However, your horse's breeding is completely irrelevant if the poor thing can't tolerate cattle.

You would think that horses and cattle would get along, in a similarly minded, herd-oriented prey animal sort of way. But cows smell funny, and they make weird noises, and there are some horses that will refuse to share their space with them for any significant amount of time. I had one horse who, despite boldly jumping over giant cross country courses and the fence line of his pasture to go exploring, would spook so significantly at the mere whiff of a nearby cow that his soul would appear to leave his body. Some horses are just not interested in interspecies activities.

However, if you are blessed with a horse that enjoys playing with other farm animals, cattle events are always a treat. Regardless of the particular sport practiced under this broad term, riding with cows requires horse and rider to work together to outwit the cow and control it's actions.

Penning, for example, involves separating several cows from the herd and moving them into a separate pen without losing control of the herd. Sorting involves finding specifically numbered cattle in a herd and working them into isolation away from the herd. Cow Working is similar to using your horse to guide a cow through a Horsemanship pattern. Roping— as the name suggests— involves horse and rider chasing a calf and snaring it in a lariat, requiring speed, agility, precision, and impressive wrist action.

It's unfair to relegate a group of sports to a brief series of sentences, especially when cow horses represent a very important part of American heritage. In fact, horses are still an important part of working ranch life, even today.

Still, not everyone has the opportunity to try cattle events because of the specific requirements involved; specifically, the cattle portion. If you are interested in working cattle, you might need to search a little harder for a trainer and opportunities to learn, depending on your location. Of course, you could substitute goats, as they do at many rodeos, but then you have to get the goat to agree to your shenanigans!

Western Roundup
Western riding is popular not only for the comfortable saddles and the glitz of the show pen but for all of the opportunities to ride a diverse number of different disciplines and styles. Though there may be overlap in some instances such as the intense variety of pattern-based classes, each Western sport has been designed to test the mental and physical athleticism of both horse and rider.
The difference in dynamic between Western riding versus English is truly fascinating. Both were born out of tradition and necessity. Western disciplines celebrate the working tradition of the ranch, while English disciplines are based on hunting across the wild countryside and military movements. Still, the overall principles are the same: accuracy, collaboration, and a true sense of communication between horse and rider.

Now let's take a look at some of the sports that don't fall specifically under "English" or "Western" riding but that still provide plenty of opportunity for engagement and development between you and your horse.

SECTION 3 : FUN FOR EVERYONE

I would like to start this section with an apology: for those who ride the following disciplines, I am sorry they haven't received as large a chunk of the book as the English and Western sports.

I appreciate all equestrian sports equally, and I think it's a shame when you've trained your entire life, only to be relegated to a short sentence or footnote in a book about horses. Realistically, each activity and subsection of this book deserves its own book in order to fully reveal and discuss the complexities and rewards of participating in that particular sport. However, my task has been to provide a brief overview to pique your interest or help you decide you're definitely not getting involved with a sport that doesn't fit you and your horse's goals very well.

I started with English and Western disciplines because they are prevalent in training barns across the United States. If you conduct an online search for "riding stable near me," you'll likely see descriptions that lead with "Western riding style," or "focus on hunter jumper training." I want to set you up with the information you'll need to navigate these descriptions as well as find your footing for progressing through the discipline you'd like to explore further.

So what are the sports that don't fit the English/Western dichotomy? Are they rogue outliers representing some type of equine anarchy? Not quite. Every type of equestrian interaction is descended from long-running tradition based on the very reasons we domesticated horses in the first place. Though we do not rely on horses for work purposes as much as we once did, we're still inexplicably drawn to the sports and activities that bring us closer to these majestic animals; Therefore, I would like to apologize to anyone who's equestrian sport of choice is not adequately represented here.

Though I have merely skimmed over a few disciplines, I have included reference material in the "Resources" section about as many opportunities for equine interaction as I could find. Look for these under the "Other Sports and Activities" section.

There are a few specific disciplines that I'd like to highlight, as I believe they are fundamental and available to a wide variety of equestrians around the world, including enjoying your gaited horse, riding out of the ring on trails, driving, and taking part in in-hand sports. Take a look to see if you and your horse might enjoy some of these options.

Saddleseat and Gaited Horses

I would love to get into the differences between the various Gaited Horse and Saddleseat disciplines and how Western pleasure has different rules and expectations when at a sponsored breed show, such as the American Morgan Horse Association (AMHA) or the Arabian Horse Association (AHA). I could spend pages regaling new equestrians about the finer points of the five-gaited Saddlebred versus the three-gaited Saddlebred.

However, these disciplines require very specific horses. The term "gaited horse" describes any equine who naturally performs gaits beyond the recognized walk, trot/jog, or canter/lope. Standardbreds may possess the ability to pace or move in such a way that both legs on each side of the body move at once, creating a lateral gait similar to the trot. Paso Fino horses have a variety of gaits that involve rapid footfalls but very little forward movement. Saddlebreds, Tennessee Walkers, Missouri Fox Trotters, and Icelandic, Hackey, and Rocky Mountain horses are just a few examples of gaited horses commonly found in the United States. Unfortunately, these gaits are innate, meaning they come from years of keen breeding. You can't really train a Thoroughbred or a Quarter Horse to perform these gaits.

There is no universal way to ride a gaited horse. The rider's attire and tack used varies depending on the type of activity being performed. Many gaited horse shows include classes that sound familiar such as Horsemanship, dressage, or hunt seat equitation. However, the structure of the class has been updated to showcase the horse's unique gaits, which are not usually demonstrated in non-gaited versions of these activities.

It's also important to note that gaited horses can do far more than gait around in circles. Gaited horses can be ridden in an English or Western saddle, or no saddle at all! I've met several gaited horses who have competed successfully in non-breed specific events, such as three day eventing, western dressage, and trail.

You may wish to work with a trainer who specializes in gaited horses; however, keep in mind that you have the freedom to do whatever you want with your horse as long as it's safe and makes both of you happy!

Going the Distance

Perhaps riding your horse in a ring or arena isn't possible or even desirable. Maybe you and your horse were designed to explore the trails less taken.

There are a variety of activities that require nothing more than a trail or an open area to explore. Endurance, Trail Riding, and Competitive Trail Riding are just a few of the equine sports that test the horse and rider's ability to not only function out in the open, but excel and thrive.

Endurance is not just the name of an equine sport— it's the main quality both horse and rider need to display to practice or compete successfully. These races take place over courses of fifty to one hundred mile distances, though limited distance rides of twenty-five to thirty-five miles are offered. This means navigating your horse over variable terrain for an entire day and pausing at regulated intervals for rest holds, during which the horse's vital signs are taken to ensure the long hike isn't having an adverse effect on him.

"The World's Best Known and Most Difficult Equestrian Endurance Ride" is the Tevis Cup, according to their promotional material. Hosted by the Western States Trail Foundation since 1955, this endurance ride covers one hundred miles of ground in just one day, including a hike up Cougar Rock, which is famous for requiring a near-vertical climb.

Of course, not every Endurance competition is held in the Rocky Mountains. Many are hosted on flat land, and riders are asked to navigate a series of loops through a small trail system. These trails are usually marked, but riders are encouraged to take a map and know basic orientation just in case a trail marker wanders off in the wind or weather.

If riding out on the trails in a competitive manner sounds like a good time, but you're not sure you have a full day of equine mountain climbing in you, perhaps Competitive Trail Riding is more your speed– literally.

Competitive Trail Riding, or CTR, is specifically not a race and is open to all riders above age 10, and horses of all breeds. Riders are expected to pace themselves through the course, generally moving no faster than 6 miles per hour. Several veterinary checks are performed throughout the ride and awards are given to the horse who is in the best overall condition once the ride has concluded.

While on the trail, the goal of CTR is to navigate the mapped course while performing certain judged tasks or obstacles, such as mounting your horse from the surrounding terrain, climbing up and down hills, stepping over logs or through water crossings, and backing up at a judge's request. It's important to remember you are not in a hurry; therefore, you can take your time setting up for each of these tasks.

Though CTR is a judged event, it is designed as more of a social activity for equestrians, much like field hunting. Riders are encouraged to help each other out and keep an eye on each other while they're out on the course, and local and regional CTR group members are often fantastic friends in addition to being fierce competitors.

However, you may not want the added pressure of being judged while you trail ride your horse. Great news: You are absolutely encouraged to ride your horse on the trails with friends and family. Riding alone on the trails is not recommended for novice riders simply due to the increased risk of the unknown on the trails. Despite the slow pace of a trail ride, you still need to have a stable seat, functional equitation, and clear communication between horse and rider.

If you do decide to ride alone, wear thick boots, pants, and a helmet, and take plenty of water and your phone with you in case of emergency. Your horse may be a really swell guy, but there are situations you may encounter on the trail that you might not have considered before. For example, during Red's first trail ride, a branch that had been broken in a recent wind storm jarred loose and dropped directly on his head. He spooked and spun around to gallop back to the trailer, dumping my trainer in the process. That's a fair reaction to the situation, but had his stablemates not been there to convince him to stay, my trainer may have had a long and painful walk through the woods in an attempt to locate my horse. Danger is quite literally everywhere on the trails, which is why some people gravitate towards the relative perceived safety of the arena.

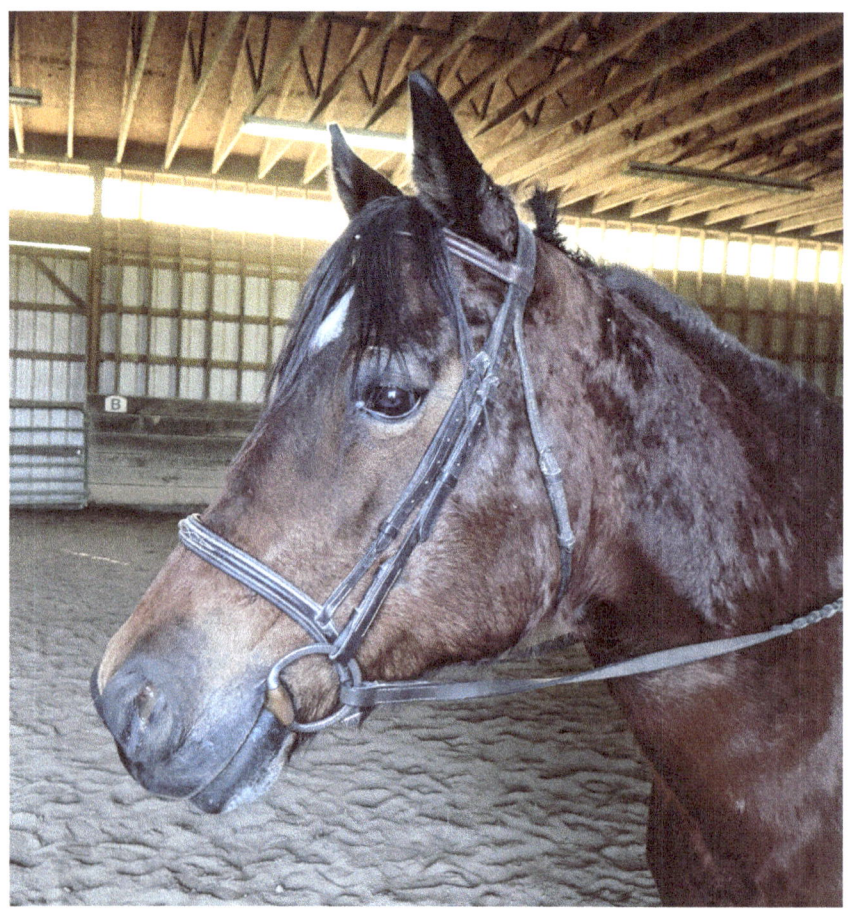

That being said, I truly hope each and every person reading this book has the experience of seeing the world between a horse's ears someday. I've had the pleasure of riding in national parks across the American West, including a memorable ride through the Tetons on a horse that had just arrived in Wyoming two days before. It might be more fair to call that an endurance ride, though, because we were traveling awfully fast for most of it!

If you'd like to test the strength of your communication skills with your horse, I strongly recommend finding your way out to a trail system. Make sure the trails are approved for equine use before you trailer out to the site, and be sure to pack plenty of water for both you and your horse. Who knows— this little ride through the woods might spark a lifelong passion for exploring!

A Different View Between the Horse's Ears

How about driving? While driving a horse remains one of my "bucket list" goals, the various things horses can do in harness is absolutely fascinating. When you ride a horse, you communicate with your hands, arms, shoulders, back, seat, and legs. When you drive a horse, you communicate through reins, a whip, and your voice.

Like trail riding, any breed of horse can participate in Carriage Driving sports. Miniature horses are extremely popular in the driving world, as they're perfectly sized to cart around a novice driver of nearly any age.

Just like the mounted sports, the athletic requirements of Carriage Driving depend on the sport practiced. Nearly everything a rider can do can be accomplished as a driver. Pleasure Driving, much like Horsemanship, involves navigating the horse through a course of maneuvers— in this case marked with cones topped with balls. While making turns, going forward, and backing up, a fault is incurred when a ball topples off of its cone.

Combined Driving is parallel to Three Day Eventing, as riders compete in three separate tests: Dressage, Marathon, and Obstacle Driving. Dressage includes a test comprised of movements that largely mirror that of classical and Western Dressage. The Marathon phase requires teams to navigate a cross country obstacle course that involves completing hills, water crossings, and a labyrinth in the quickest time. Obstacle Driving asks teams to pass through up to twenty "gates," which are pairs of cones and balls set up so drivers must guide the horse and carriage through them swiftly and without disturbing the balls, much as a stadium jump course asks riders not to knock the poles off of the fences they jump.

There are also many arena driving classes, in which pairs of horse and rider drive along the rail to impress the judges with their spectacular turnout, expressive horse, and overall compliance with the image of a cheerful carriage ride on a sunny day.

When putting your horse in harness, I strongly recommend a trainer who has started horses in the lines before, especially if your equine companion has never done this. Some horses protest to things being behind their hindquarters, while others are unfamiliar with the feeling of something dragging behind them. From there, however, the world of driven events opens up, with options like skijoring in the snow or taking friends and family for pony cart rides on the front lawn.

You Don't Have to Ride

I've mentioned this several times throughout this book, but it bears mentioning on its own:

You don't have to ride to enjoy your horse.

There are many activities that allow you to participate with your horse in-hand, or on a lead rope, instead of in the saddle or behind the harness. The groundwork we discussed in the first part of this book can be the start and end point for your work with your horse.

At shows, you can find in-hand classes. Halter and Showmanship allow horse and human combinations to show off conformation and communication equally as the handler asks the horse to perform various movements at the request of the judge. There may be a pattern to work as well, generally consisting only of walk and trot movements, with some halted pivots or turns and backing up a few steps.

To add a little zest to the equation, in-hand trail classes ask riders to perform over, around, and through many of the obstacles found in a Mounted Trail class. It's not a simple matter of having your horse follow you around the arena, though. Horses are expected to travel with their left shoulder aligned with the handler's right shoulder regardless of which in-hand class they choose, which means sharing the same space. As a result, the handlers and horses must have the ability to communicate clearly with each other to avoid collisions over poles or squeezing through gates.

While commonly associated with younger horses, every equestrian should try out the concepts of in-hand trail, especially when in the introductory stage of getting to know your horse. You can use basic PVC poles or even pool noodles to create low-cost obstacles and use one of the online patterns as your guide. Mounted Trail patterns can also be adapted to in-hand trail use by eliminating the lope.

There are so many things to do with horses that I hope to eventually write a book to dig deeper into each activity. However, I hope this brief overview has provided you with enough inspiration to encourage you to check out a few new things to try with your horse.

Even if you don't pursue any of these activities professionally, applying the basics to your next work session can really make a difference in your ability to communicate with your horse. You may not want to switch things up until you and your horse have really hit your stride— literally and figuratively— though remember, there's no shame in starting at the very beginning and working your way towards the more advanced levels with practice.

In fact, starting with a basic, "Hello," and building towards your short and long-term goals is exactly the type of relationship I would recommend you establish with your horse. I also encourage you to let the process take as long as it needs for both you and your horse to feel completely comfortable forging forward.

CONCLUSION

In conclusion, respect your horse. Spend time with him. Learn how to talk not just at him, but with him. Find things the two of you can do together that you both enjoy, and appreciate each and every moment you have together... even if you sometimes wish your horse could spend the night at Grandma's house when he acts up.

When I say, "Love your horse," I don't necessarily mean hugging, kissing, and professing your undying affection for him every single day, though by all means, feel free to do just that. Instead, I encourage you to build an affectionate bond with him. Earlier, I referred to this as a "good working relationship," and that's exactly what you should strive towards.

Consider your horse as you would your coworkers. At your jobsite, you may find colleagues with whom you have an instant bond. You have similar interests or sensibilities, and you love hanging out beyond the workplace. There is also that special breed of coworker with whom you don't mind having a meal or happy hour celebration with, but you probably wouldn't invite them to your wedding. Then, you have the coworkers with whom you are able to accomplish great things in the office, but it would never occur to you to invite them to lunch.

Many people believe that they must have the type of bond with their horse that makes them super besties no matter what they're doing. In all reality, not all horse-human bonds work out that way. That doesn't mean you've failed. In my own life, I've had the privilege of working with a full kaleidoscope of equine personalities. I've had horses who love to snuggle, and I've had horses who were almost offended when I patted them with affection. The physical and emotional aspects of the relationship aren't measured in the same way as what the two of you can accomplish together.

That being said, one of your goals may be to find your heart horse. The term "heart horse" has been coined to describe a horse who is you in horse form. The legend goes that every equestrian has at least one heart horse, with whom they bond instantly and on an entirely different level than any other horse. From experience, I can tell you that this is a real phenomenon. From the moment I slipped a halter on Red's skinny face, I knew that we were already on the same page. Communicating with your heart horse is almost instantaneous; cooperation is a different story, however.

Earlier, we talked about what to do if your horse doesn't like you. I explained that horses generally don't dislike people without reason. Now that you've read this book, I suggest that you reframe the concept. It's likely not *you* that the horse doesn't like, so much as what you're *doing.* That can range from dislike of the brush you're using at a particular moment, to a general distaste for the discipline you're currently schooling. If your horse is communicating to you that he's cranky, bored, or uncomfortable, try something else.

And now you have a whole range of "something elses" to try. The second section of this book focused on the various things that can be done with horses, and as I've admitted, I barely managed to skim the first layer of detail. Equestrian sports are some of the oldest athletic activities on this planet. Born from human need, each sport has developed into a test of a horse and handler's ability to communicate and accomplish great things together. I encourage everyone to check out the "Resources" section at the end of this book to help you and your horse safely and correctly navigate the waters that come with learning about a new horse. I strongly recommend at least learning the fundamentals from a professional in the discipline that intrigues you so that you're aware of how to safely and correctly practice your chosen activity for a long time.

You don't need to ever walk in the show ring to be successful at these disciplines, either. You may choose to go to fun shows, where the only requirement is a helmet and boots, or aim for events that cost money and earn you points on the circuit. The gauge of success isn't ribbons, trophies, or medals, but in how much enjoyment you and your horse get from your activities. Yes, it's very nice to have a physical manifestation of your ability to cooperate with a 1,000-pound prey animal, but the real accomplishment is the cooperation itself. At the end of the day, a ribbon is just a bit of fabric, and a trophy is just some metal. Points are arbitrary and usually expire at the end of a season. The thrill and serenity that comes from that working relationship with a horse, however? That lasts a lifetime.

Enjoy your horse, and tell him I send my regards!

RESOURCES

The internet has a seemingly infinite amount of information about absolutely anything horse-related. It should go without saying that not all of this information is of the same quality or accuracy. Additionally, different trainers will have different perspectives on what success looks like, as their formula for training has been carefully developed through their own experiences. That is to say, every trainer is going to feel that their recipe for winning is the "correct" method.

Therefore, I've done my best to collect unbiased resources that can provide you with further information on the topics discussed in this book. Please don't consider these endorsements of any kind, but rather a gathering of launch pads from which you can find your own rabbit hole. I've tried to include official websites wherever possible to ensure that you're starting with the official word on each matter.

I'm not personally affiliated with any breed or sport organization, either. Belle is registered with AQHA, but as I don't intend to show or breed her, that's mainly to establish and maintain my rights as her legal owner. Red is registered through the Jockey Club, and though his registry rights were never transferred to me, his purchase was documented through an agent for his previous owner.

As you read these, please don't consider them a personal endorsement, as I get no kickback or benefit from these sites or links. Instead, understand that I considered these very thorough and comprehensive guides to help you get settled on the path to happiness with your equine companion.

Enjoy!

Bonding and Communication Work

The following links lead to groundwork and communication exercises for horse and human. Though I mention these exercises in the context of introducing yourself to your horse, remember that you can step back and refresh your communication skills with your horse at any time.

As I mentioned, each expert has a different methodology, so I've attempted to bring you a variety of perspectives in the following sites:

Monty Roberts : https://montyroberts.com/

Clinton Anderson: https://downunderhorsemanship.com/

Warwick Schiller: https://www.warwickschiller.com/

Craig Cameron: https://craigcameron.com/

Jim Thomas: http://barthorsemanship.com/

Exercises:

https://equinehelper.com/5-best-groundwork-exercises-for-your-horse/

https://www.youtube.com/watch?v=YZFjsf5t0cM

https://www.youtube.com/watch?v=n0kVp4oU8Q8

English Riding

The following sites and videos will help provide a visual to complement what you've just read, in addition to providing you with your first stepping stone through the doorway of hunt seat riding sports.

Riding on the Flat

Lynn Palm: http://www.lynnpalm.com/

Note: Ms. Palm is also a fantastic resource on the matter of Western Dressage, should you find interest in that topic, as well.

USEF: https://www.usef.org/compete/disciplines/hunter-seat-equitation

US Pony Club: https://www.ponyclub.org/Members/Disciplines/HunterSeatEquitation/

Videos:

https://www.youtube.com/watch?v=atvDIXPTmKg

https://www.youtube.com/watch?v=oxWHHigKW1E

Show Jumping

USEF: https://www.usef.org/compete/disciplines/jumping

Understanding Courses: https://www.horsejournals.com/riding-training/english/hunter-jumper/how-walk-jump-course

US Pony Club: https://www.ponyclub.org/members/disciplines/showjumping/

Videos:

https://www.youtube.com/watch?v=eT1WygNY0n8

https://www.youtube.com/watch?v=d4PyKUqR96Q

Cross Country / Three Day Eventing

USEF: https://www.usef.org/compete/disciplines/eventing

Dressage: https://useventing.com/events-competitions/resources/dressage-tests

Cross Country:https://horseandcountry.tv/en-us/cross-country-horse-riding-for-beginners/

Stadium: https://useventing.com/resources/documents/The-Basics-of-Jumping-Course-Design-for-Eventing.pdf

Videos:

"The Event Formerly known as Rolex" is one of the top Three-Day Events in the world. Currently known as the Land Rover Kentucky Three Day Event, you can see some of the top riders in the sport on this course:

https://www.youtube.com/watch?v=TnL26YXBwt8

https://www.youtube.com/watch?v=sNRt6Od6COo

https://www.youtube.com/watch?v=DCrL580E7Zk

https://www.youtube.com/watch?v=Yc-UGH6ms5U

Field Hunting

Is Your Horse Ready?, by Old North Bridge Hounds: https://oldnorthbridge-hounds.org/2009/11/17/is-your-horse-ready-to-hunt/

MFHA: https://mfha.com/

A History in North America, from Fox Hunting Life: https://www.foxhuntinglife.com/american-foxhunting

Sidesaddle: http://www.americansidesaddleassociation.org/

Videos:

https://www.youtube.com/watch?v=-1HyfOYjJZk

https://www.youtube.com/watch?v=FXtrv11h8tE

Western Riding

The following links will help you learn more about the low and slow, precise and nice, and adrenaline-soaked versions of the style that was developed by working riders on the range.

Overview

Types of Riding: https://horserookie.com/what-are-different-types-western-riding/

Pleasure

AQHA: https://www.aqha.com/western-pleasure

A History: http://www.parksonline.org/equestrians/sports/western01.html

The Basics: https://www.horsejournals.com/riding-training/western/western-pleasure/basics-showing-western-pleasure

Videos:

https://www.youtube.com/watch?v=Bb7kN6jaKps

https://www.youtube.com/watch?v=vRywYlwIIEk

Horsemanship

Patterns: https://www.aqha.com/-/13-aqha-horsemanship-patterns-for-you-to-practice

How To: https://www.horseillustrated.com/horse-exclusives-horsemanship-pattern

AQHA: https://www.aqha.com/-/horse-showing-in-a-pattern-class

Videos:

https://www.youtube.com/watch?v=PwGi8m1gHvo

Equal parts informative and video: https://horses.extension.org/judging-horse-events-western-horsemanship/

Trail

Trail Obstacles: https://trailriderchallenge.com/trc-explained/obstacles/

AQHA: https://www.aqha.com/trail

Trail Patterns: http://www.showhorsepromotions.com/trailpatterns.htm

Videos:

https://www.youtube.com/watch?v=tYnQpa5TN1g

https://www.youtube.com/watch?v=OPVSkSt5c6g&t=188s

Ranch Riding

AQHA: https://www.aqha.com/ranch-riding1

Patterns: https://www.aqha.com/aqha-show-patterns

Please note- this link includes direction to all AQHA patterns, including other disciplines and sports. You can explore them all from the menu.

How To: https://www.farnam.com/stable-talk/maximize-your-scores-in-ranch-riding

Videos:

https://www.youtube.com/watch?v=Z8p4ybBsFY8

https://www.youtube.com/watch?v=26TyQ9lcXIg

Western Dressage

WDAA: https://www.westerndressageassociation.org/

Western Dressage Tests: https://wdaa.memberclicks.net/wdaa-tests

USEF: https://www.usef.org/compete/disciplines/western-dressage

Videos:

https://www.youtube.com/watch?v=ClHuAg9RNOw

https://www.youtube.com/watch?v=xe4-LIKHN2w

Reining

NRHA Patterns: https://nrha.com/media/pdf/2017/patterns.pdf

FEI: https://www.fei.org/stories/sport/reining/everything-you-need-know-about-reining

AQHA: https://www.aqha.com/-/seven-tips-for-stepping-up-your-reining-game

Videos:

https://www.youtube.com/watch?v=cqbYdyTbODE

https://www.youtube.com/watch?v=4YCgsZmjsww

Speed Events

Kristin Weaver Brown: http://kristinweaverbrown.com/

NBHA: https://nbha.com/

Gymkhana: https://timetoride.org/riders/about-horses/horse-activities/contesting-gymkhana/

Gymkhana Games: https://horseyhooves.com/mounted-horse-games/

Videos:

https://www.youtube.com/watch?v=n0Qk5tsJz4o

https://www.youtube.com/watch?v=ibvovCudG_s

Cowboy Mounted Shooting

CMSA: https://www.cmsaevents.com/about/

AQHA: https://www.aqha.com/-/give-it-a-shot-part-1

Videos:

https://www.youtube.com/watch?v=XBsr4aT7tmA

https://www.youtube.com/watch?v=YO5B8zR7F3c

Cattle Events

Cattle Events Explained: https://www.horseillustrated.com/category/riding-and-training/disciplines/cattle-events

Reined Cow Horse: https://nrcha.com/affiliate-events/

Working Cow Horse: https://www.aqha.com/working-cow-horse

Cutting: https://nchacutting.com/

Roping: https://equinewellnessmagazine.com/horse-roping/

Videos:

https://www.youtube.com/watch?v=6g4f9gxGO9Y

https://www.youtube.com/watch?v=nUZ2gxcBHBo

Other Sports and Activities

Saddle Seat

Understanding the Sport: https://www.horseillustrated.com/horse-exclusives-saddleseat-judge-myths

USEF: https://www.usef.org/compete/disciplines/saddle-seat/usa-saddle-seat

US Saddle Seat: https://www.ussaddleseat.com/

Videos:

https://www.youtube.com/watch?v=15cHhqvevT4

https://www.youtube.com/watch?v=X_7z8pvqXPc

Endurance

AERC: https://www.aerc.org/

FEI: https://www.fei.org/endurance

Tevis Cup: http://www.teviscup.org/

Videos:

https://www.youtube.com/watch?v=MWsi1Uc_MbA

https://www.youtube.com/watch?v=s2J-3j8ueoo

Trail Riding and Competitive Trail Riding

NATRC: https://www.natrc.org/

Trail Riding Safety: https://horseandrider.com/trail-riding/trail-riding-safety-tips-15710

How To: https://equusmagazine.com/riding/build-trustworthy-trail-horse-10655/

Videos:

https://www.youtube.com/watch?v=Ti5wfyD_kIo

https://www.youtube.com/watch?v=pVP3xwkeS2M

Driving

World Horse Driving Association: https://www.worldhorsedriving.com/competition-info#:~:text=September%202021-,About%20the%20sport,dressage%2C%20marathon%20and%20obstacle%20driving.

General Driving Information: http://www.theshowring.info/Driving.htm

US Equestrian Carriage Driving Guide: https://www.usequestrian.org/compete/resources-forms/disciplines/carriage-pleasure-driving

https://www.americandrivingsociety.org/content.aspx?page_id=22&club_id=548049&module_id=407752

Videos:

https://www.youtube.com/watch?v=owwwmdc6S-M

https://www.youtube.com/watch?v=eNKOsd-zKd4

Halter and In-Hand

Halter:

https://www.horseillustrated.com/horse-showing-how-to-show-in-halter-classes

Showmanship: https://www.horseillustrated.com/western-horse-training-showmanship-dos-and-donts

In-Hand Trail:

https://passionatehorsemanship.com/8499/difference-between-horse-agility-and-in-hand-trail-or-halter-obstacle/

Videos:

https://www.youtube.com/watch?v=NrvU0YcdtEU

https://www.youtube.com/watch?v=l8bcetss8SM

Polo

Though not mentioned in the main text, Polo is a thrilling sport in which horse and rider chase a ball with mallets in the pursuit of whacking the ball into a goal. Not entirely unlike the Quidditch tournaments made popular in J.K. Rowling's *Harry Potter* series, Polo is fast-paced and requires infinite concentration as well as the abilities of any superstar athlete.

https://www.uspolo.org/

Skijoring

I did, in fact, mention this activity in the text, but I didn't provide an explanation. When executed improperly, skijoring can be a very bad idea. However, I will include a link so that you can find safe and enjoyable ways to try this Nordic sport.

http://www.skijorinternational.com/the-history

Breed Organizations

This is another area in which I will need to apologize for limiting myself. There are many horse breeds, all of which are quite amazing. The following list is simply recognition of the breeds specifically mentioned in this book, in case you wanted to learn more about each breed mentioned.

Thoroughbred: https://www.jockeyclub.com

American Quarter Horse: www.aqha.com

Lipizzaner: https://www.uslipizzan.org/

Appaloosa: https://www.appaloosa.com/

Paint Horse: https://apha.com/

Arabian: https://www.arabianhorses.org/

Hackney: http://hackneysociety.com/

Saddlebred: https://www.asha.net/

Tennessee Walker: https://twhbea.com/, https://nwha.com/

Missouri Fox Trotter: https://mfthba.com/

Icelandic: https://icelandics.org/

Morgan: https://www.morganhorse.com/

Rocky Mountain Horse: https://www.rmhorse.com/

Paso Fino: https://www.pfha.org/

REVIEWS

Reviews and feedback help improve this book and the author. If you enjoy this book, we would greatly appreciate it if you could take a few moments to share your opinion and post a review on Amazon.

ALSO BY MEREDITH HILL

Before Your Horse Comes Home

Finding Your First Horse

www.ingramcontent.com/pod-product-compliance
Lightning Source LLC
Chambersburg PA
CBHW071420070526
44578CB00003B/625